The
Gift
of the
Gospel

BASIC TEACHINGS
of the CHRISTIAN FAITH

H. Gerard Knoche

Augsburg
MINNEAPOLIS

THE GIFT OF THE GOSPEL
Basic Teachings of the Christian Faith

Cover and interior design by MacLean and Tuminelly

Library of Congress Cataloging-in-Publication Data

Knoche, H. Gerard
    The gift of the gospel : basic teachings of the Christian faith /
H. Gerard Knoche.
        p.   cm.
    Includes bibliographical references (p.   ).
    ISBN 0-8066-2783-2 (alk. paper)
    1. Faith   2. Theology, Doctrinal   I. Title.
BT771.2.K59 1995
230—dc20   95-30561
                                                                CIP

The paper used in this publication meets the minimum requirements of American National Standard for Information Sciences—Permanence of Paper for Printed Library Materials, ANSI Z329.48-1984.   (∞)™

Manufactured in the U.S.A.   AF 9-2783

99   98   97   96   95   1   2   3   4   5   6   7   8   9   10

Contents

Author's Note

In these times when justice requires that we reshape language referring to people to be gender inclusive, an author who wants to draw upon writers from earlier periods is left with a dilemma. Though writers of previous times were not sensitive to this issue, I have tried to provide gender inclusive translations when appropriate. However, when such translations were not available, I inserted inclusive words in brackets wherever the original language would not be perceived as inclusive today. Unfortunately, I know of no neuter terms. Many illustrations talk about individual men and use male imagery, and I hope readers will be able to regard these illustrations as what they are and find them helpful regardless of the exclusive language used.

H. Gerard Knoche

Preface

We live in an increasingly secular society where knowledge of religion cannot be taken for granted. As a pastor, I am asked, "I'm dating a Christian and know nothing about Christianity. Can you tell me what a Christian is?" Ten years ago that never would have happened. It is no longer accurate to assume that because someone is an American that he or she will also be knowledgeable about Christianity.

Among those who do call themselves Christians, education about what they believe often stops at confirmation. What they learned then does not seem adequate to answer the questions they now have as adults. Nor is it adequate to help them answer the honest questions others have about Christianity.

The Gift of the Gospel provides, first, a clear, short explanation of the Christian faith for those who have never learned about it and, second, an adult presentation of Christianity for those who want to reexamine the faith of their youth.

Like the gospel, this book is in many ways a gift. Few of the ideas are new. The stories and illustrations are ones I have collected through the years because they were helpful to me. For the faithful witnesses who have preserved and interpreted the tradition and handed it on to me, I give thanks. Rarely have I been so aware of how much of what I perceive as my own understanding of the faith has been assimilated from others. I have tried to give credit for those ideas for which I could recall or discover the source, and I apologize for anything for which I seem to take credit that originated with someone else.

This book is a gift that passes on to others the gifts I have received. It is more valuable than any other gift I have ever given, for the gift of the gospel is the gift I would most like to share.

Introduction

"For by grace you have been saved through faith, and this is not your own doing; it is the gift of God—not the result of works, so that no one may boast" (Ephesians 2:8–9).

For years I had trouble accepting gifts—at least those that were labeled as such. All sorts of thoughts would rush through my mind whenever someone surprised me with a present. "I really don't deserve it." "I can't afford to pay her back." "Why didn't I think to get something for him?" "She can't afford to give me this." I had similar feelings at Christmas and on birthdays, but I had learned to moderate them by being sure to have a gift on the appropriate occasion for everyone who gave to me. Thus giving became a form of trading.

Then a critical question arose: If I was not able to accept gifts gracefully from others, could I honestly say I could accept things from God? Aware that salvation itself was a gift and that the bread and wine received in Holy Communion each week were one part of that gift, I knew that I was not dealing with an issue on the periphery of faith. Being able to receive gifts is a requisite for receiving the gospel.

Fundamental to my difficulty of receiving gifts was my discomfort with being in debt to someone. An unexpected gift was a sign that I had lost control of that relationship. I had a strong streak in me that said it was important to be able to say I had earned what I received. As long as that was true, I was in control of my self-concept and of my destiny. As long as I didn't fail, this system worked.

Only after a personal failure that demonstrated clearly what an illusion it is to believe that my life is in any way in my control have I begun to be gracious about receiving gifts from others and from God. I have learned not only that gifts themselves are the expressions of love, but that one expresses love by receiving them joyfully.

Swiss psychiatrist Paul Tournier generalized this experience. He said, "[People] need to give because they need to give themselves, and all their gifts are signs of that deep-seated universal desire to give oneself.... The meaning of gifts is in the love they express, the love both given and received."[1] Not to receive a gift is to keep others, as well as oneself, from expressing an essential part of humanity.

Henri Nouwen went a step further when he said that the capacity to receive gifts, the posture of standing with open hands, is necessary if we want to communicate with God. "The challenge of the gospel," he wrote, "lies precisely in the invitation to accept a gift for which we can give nothing in return."[2] To accept a gift from God is to acknowledge that God is in control of that for which we most desperately long.

Out of this personal experience I have come to organize this presentation of the message of the Christian faith around the theme of gifts. After beginning with an examination of the giver, God, and what we can know about God (chapter 1), we look at the receiver and cover the doctrines of humanity and sin (chapter 2). Then in chapter 3 we will examine the gift itself, salvation, from a number of perspectives. In chapter 4 we will consider the response to the gift through ethics and social ministry. We will then look at the community of the gifted (chapter 5), one translation of the nature of the church. Included in this section will be a discussion of the sacraments. In chapter six we will see how the relationship with God is tended and nourished. In chapter 7 we will look at the last gifts: Jesus' return, the last judgment, and life everlasting.

Chapter 8 deals with the question of how we know the Christian story of the gift of the gospel is true. Others have considered revelation as a starting point. I find few people who in actual practice begin to enter the community of faith by agreeing with a doctrine of authority of the Bible. Such authority was always assumed by Jesus and never debated. If Scripture is self-authenticating, as Luther suggested, then one should tell its story and not argue early for its authority. Or, in the metaphor of this discussion, one rarely doubts the genuineness of the gift before discovering what it is.

My approach to Christian faith takes "grace," the unmerited gift of God, as the organizing principle. There was a time when to do so would be to encourage the growth of an illusion that Christianity was all benefits and no responsibility, all crown and no cross.[3] My contention is that in our time there is such an inundation of bad news daily that we need to hear good news as clearly and simply as we dare present it. In a time when there is a general feeling of hopelessness about the capability to modify the sad prospects ahead, we need to hear about God the giver, whose power to give good gifts has not been eroded or made contingent on our efforts. In a time when the worldwide economy is faltering and people do without, news about the free gift of God should have an eager audience.

I chose "grace," or gift, as a focus for the gospel because such a choice is faithful to the biblical tradition. If John 3:16 ("For God so loved the world that he gave his only Son, so that everyone who believes in him may not perish but may have eternal life") is a summary of the gospel, then the gospel is about what God gave. The theme of God's giving and our receiving is repeated throughout the Gospel of John. In Romans 6, Paul contrasted life under the law and its benefits with "the free gift of God," which is the new covenant. Generosity is the chief virtue of the new being, the one turned away from preoccupation with self into a person-for-others.

— 1 —

The Giver

"Every generous act of giving, with every perfect gift, is from above, coming down from the Father of lights, with whom there is no variation or shadow due to change" (James 1:17).

In these words from J. D. Salinger's novel *Franny and Zooey*, Zooey provides one answer to the question "Who is Jesus?"—an answer that was formulated on the basis of his reading of the Bible:

The part that stumps me, really stumps me, is that I can't see why anybody . . . would even want to say a prayer to a Jesus who was the least bit different from the way he looks and sounds in the New Testament. He's only the most intelligent man in the Bible, that's all. Who isn't he head and shoulders over? Who? Both testaments are full of prophets, disciples, favorite sons, Solomons, Davids, Isaiahs, Pauls but, my God, who besides Jesus really knew which end was up? Not Moses. Don't tell me Moses. He was a nice man, and he kept in beautiful touch with God and all that—but that's exactly the point. He had to keep in touch. Jesus realizes that there was no separation from God.... Who else, for example, would have kept his mouth shut when Pilate asked for an explanation? Not Solomon. Don't say Solomon. Solomon would have had a few pithy words for the occasion. I'm not sure Socrates wouldn't have, for that matter. Crito, or somebody, would have managed to pull him aside just long enough to get a few well-chosen words for the record.... Besides everything else, who in the Bible besides Jesus knew—*knew*—that we're carrying the kingdom of heaven around with us—inside—where we're all too stupid and sentimental and unimaginative to look? You have to be the Son of God to know that kind of stuff. Jesus was a supreme *adept*, by God, on a terribly important mission. This was no St. Francis with enough time to knock off a few canticles and preach to the birds…. If God had wanted somebody with St. Francis' winning personality for the job in the New Testament, he'd have picked him, you can be sure. As it was he picked the best, the smartest, the most loving, the least sentimental, the most unimitative master he could have picked.[1]

The Giver of the gift of salvation is God. The clearest picture of God that has been provided for us is in Jesus Christ. Jesus is a window up to God and a mirror up to humanity. While God was revealed long ago "in many and various ways by the prophets" (Hebrews 1:1), God's most complete self-disclosure is in the person of Jesus Christ. Martin Luther's explanation of the Second Article of the Apostles' Creed begins, "I believe that Jesus Christ—true God, Son of the Father from eternity, and true man, born of the Virgin Mary—is my Lord."[2] If we want to know what God is like, we need to look at Jesus.

The Incarnation

God is revealed in Jesus, first of all, to be *personal*. When the book of Genesis says we are created in God's image, part of what is being asserted is that God is like us in that God has personality. There is no question historically that Jesus lived as a first-century Palestinian. By being personal, God also makes it possible for us to know God in ways analogous to the ways we know others. God is not a metaphysical idea. The traditional arguments for the existence of God tell us there is a great design to the universe, so there must be a designer; there is a sense of "oughtness" about the universe, so there must be a source of good; there must be a first cause. These arguments, however, are all inadequate because none leads to a conclusion that there is a God who is personal.

Following directly from the belief that God is personal is the idea that God is *communicative*. We know about other people on the basis of our observations of them and their self-disclosure. Jesus was God's form of self-disclosure. The Gospel writer John calls him the Word of God—God's means of speaking to us. While much about God remains a mystery, God chose to make known much about the divine nature. Jesus was able to say, "Whoever has seen me has seen the Father" (John 14:9). The name the prophets gave to the coming Messiah was Immanuel, or "God with us."

Why God would choose to communicate with humanity by becoming human is made clearer by an old story. A man was walking through a pasture. He came upon an ant hill and amused himself by watching the ants as they busily scurried in and out. Then he happened to move into a position that cast his shadow over the ant hill. Immediately all activity ceased. The ants disappeared into their home. When he stepped back so that his shadow was not over the ant hill, the ants resumed their activities.

Intrigued by the ants' reactions to shadows and light, he proceeded to conduct a little experiment. Again he let his shadow fall on the hill. The ants disappeared. Then he moved away. Once more the ants became busy as soon as the shadow was gone. Evidently, they were afraid of the sudden darkness.

The man wondered how he could prove to the ants that he meant them no harm. He finally concluded that the only way he could do this successfully would be to become an ant himself. Then he could communicate with the ants. He could convince them that he wanted to be their friend.[3] Of course, no human can become an ant—but God can become human, and that is what God did.

A third thing Jesus told us about God was that God is *loving*, that God cares for humanity. God is not a disinterested judge, a moral ruler of the universe, as some religions propose. Rather, God's love was revealed in the way Jesus believed and in what he taught. The very desire of God to communicate, to be manifest in human form, is a demonstration of love. He went about healing the sick who came to him. He made friends with the transients, the poverty ridden, the sleazy characters of his time. One Gospel writer said, "When he saw the crowds, he had compassion for them, because they were harassed and helpless" (Matthew 9:36). But most of all he died an ignominious death as a criminal, when he was innocent, so that people might be reconciled to God. "No one has greater love than this, to lay down one's life for one's friends" (John 15:13), he told his disciples, and then he provided a firsthand experience of that love for them in the crucifixion.

Jesus' teachings had an accent of love new to his time. He reminded the Jews that their own legal system could be summarized by loving God and loving their neighbors. Where keeping the law had been a maximum requirement, Jesus called for people to go beyond the law by loving, turning the other cheek, giving more than others ask, going the second mile. The story of the Samaritan who helped the Jew beaten by robbers has become the classic illustration of unmerited love (Luke 10:25–37). Jesus saw himself fulfilling the law, at his Last Supper he told his disciples he had a new commandment for them: "Just as I have loved you, you also should love one another" (John 13:34).

Finally, Jesus revealed that God is *powerful* over all the forces that often seem stronger than human strength. Jesus had power over the evil forces of his time, manifested in his casting out of demons. He had power to heal the sick. He raised to life those who had died, like the children of Jairus and the widow of Nain, and especially Lazarus. He forgave sinners, a use of power that his contemporaries ultimately used as a reason for his death. They argued that only God had the power to forgive sins. Unless Jesus was in fact God, his declarations of forgiveness were blasphemy. He showed power over nature, calming the storm on the Sea of Galilee when it frightened the disciples in the boat. He even had power over the devil, resisting the devil's clever attempts to trick him.

On the third day, he rose from the dead

The ultimate revelation that God had power came in Jesus' resurrection. Others may have come back from the edge of death only to face death a second time, but Jesus was raised from the dead into a new existence, never to die again. Death, a power with which every person must cope, was no longer the victor. "Where, O death, is your victory? Where, O death, is your sting?" wrote Paul (1 Corinthians 15:55). "The third day he rose again from the dead," the creed says, and the power of God to defeat what we fear most was made manifest.

But the resurrection is more than a display of God's power. It is the central and unique occurrence in the life of Jesus upon which the validity of everything else hangs. In Paul's words, "and if Christ has not been raised, then our proclamation has been in vain and your faith has been in vain" (1 Corinthians 15:14). There has to be some criterion to test the notion that Jesus is true God. For many people the resurrection is that touchstone. Of course, its truth does not prove in a philosophical sense that Jesus is divine, but it does make that claim plausible. The evidence is quite striking.

There are five different accounts of the resurrection in the Bible, one by each of the evangelists and the oldest account, an oral tradition recorded by Paul in 1 Corinthians. This is far more, by the way, than we have to verify most other events of ancient history, the truthfulness of which we never question. On the basis of these accounts, three kinds of evidence were presented for the resurrection.

First, the tomb was empty when Mary Magdalene, Salome, and others went to further anoint the body of Jesus with spices. All four Gospels report that those who returned to the tomb found it empty and the stone rolled away.

Second, Jesus appeared to many. Paul gave one list: Cephas, the Twelve, five hundred of the fellow Christians at one time, James, and Paul himself. Luke told how Jesus surprised the disciples on the Emmaus Road. Mary Magdalene saw Jesus outside the tomb. John recorded Jesus' appearance to the skeptical Thomas in the Upper Room where the frightened disciples had gathered after the crucifixion. Jesus also appeared for breakfast on the beach with the disciples.

Finally, and most convincingly, the disciples were transformed after they saw the risen Jesus. When Jesus did not turn out to be the catalyst for the new order for which they hoped, they became so dejected and despondent that all but John deserted at Jesus' death.

But after the disciples had seen the risen Lord, they began preaching until, by the time of their deaths, the good news of God's love had been taken to all of the known world. When authorities tried to stop them, they said they must obey God rather than human authority. They were so convinced of their message that many of them died rather than compromise it.

Some who have examined the evidence reject it largely because Jesus' resurrection is a unique event in history. They begin with the presupposition, "Resurrections don't happen, so look only for alternative explanations of the evidence." As it stands, however, there is a strong case for its occurrence—a number of documents written close to the time of the event said it occurred, and no documents of that time denounced it.

Ethelbert Stauffer of Germany wrote:

> What do we do [as historians] when we experience surprises which run counter to all our expectations, perhaps all our convictions and even our period's whole understanding of truth? We say, as one great historian used to say in these instances, 'And why not? For the critical historian, nothing is impossible."[4]

A legal scholar from England made this summary:

> As a lawyer, I have made a prolonged study of the evidences for the
> events of the first Easter Day. To me the evidence is conclusive, and over
> and over again in the High Court I have secured a verdict on evidence
> not nearly so compelling. Inference follows on evidence, and a truthful
> witness is always artless and disdains effect. The gospel evidence for the
> resurrection is of this class, and as a lawyer, I accept it unreservedly as the
> testimony of truthful [people], to facts they were able to substantiate.[5]

The discussion of the resurrection began because the resurrection is
an example of God's power revealed by Jesus. It is also the unique aspect
of Christian teaching and it is pivotal in determining the credibility of
Jesus' claim to be true God. It also has ramifications in terms of the
lifestyle and future of believers.

God, the creator

Careful attention to Jesus' words make one aware that while Jesus was
all God (and fully human), he was not all of God. He prayed to the
Father and taught his disciples to do the same. He was sent by the
Father. He declared that he and the Father were one (John 10:30). At
age twelve he said that he must be about his Father's business (Luke
2:49). Both in Gethsemane and in the Upper Room during his farewell
discourse he called on his Father in prayer. Clearly the one who gives
the gift has another name—Father.

Like Jesus, the Father is primarily known on the basis of what he
does. Nowhere in the Bible are the philosophic attributes of God spelled
out. The omniscient, omnipotent, omnipresent God is an extrapolation
from the data, speculation with which Christians sometimes have been
in agreement. But even if the speculation of the philosophers is not
accepted, the Father has made himself known.

God is known, first and foremost, as the creator of all things visible
and invisible. That creation is not a one-time occurrence. This is no watch-
maker God who wound up the universe and now watches it run down. In
his explanation of the First Article of the Apostles' Creed, Luther said:

> I believe that God has created me and all that exists. He has given me
> and still preserves my body and soul with all their powers. He provides
> me with food and clothing, home and family, daily work, and all I need
> from day to day. God also protects me in time of danger and guards me

from every evil. All this he does out of fatherly and divine goodness and mercy, though I do not deserve it. Therefore I surely ought to thank and praise, serve and obey him. This is most certainly true.[6]

God's act of creation in the beginning was an act of creation out of nothing. That act is sufficient in itself to establish God as almighty, having power and mystery beyond human comprehension. How did God create such a world as ours from nothing? That we cannot know. In this way God is *transcendent*, "totally other," beyond our finding out.

But Luther's stress on the ongoingness of God's creative activity was his way of saying that this same God is *immanent*. God is concerned with the daily lives we lead. God comes among us, not just in Jesus to one time in history, but perpetually with creative and sustaining work.

If creation is one activity of God by which the deity is revealed, there are two others. To the people of Israel, God has been a deliverer and a promise-maker. As the giver, God gave deliverance and promises. Deliverance was preeminently manifest in the history of Israel in the escape from Pharaoh. God parted the Red Sea so that the people of Israel could escape Pharaoh's armies and begin the journey into the promised homeland. That deliverance remains the identity-giving event celebrated by the Jewish people as well as a sign of another deliverance yet to come through the waters of baptism into God's kingdom.

The deliverance known as the Exodus was not the only occasion when God acted as deliverer. Again and again God was given credit for Israel's victories in battle. Joshua, Gideon, and David were among the leaders who followed God's direction and were victorious. Daniel was delivered from the mouths of lions. Shadrach, Meshach, and Abednego were delivered from a fiery furnace. Finally, a small number of Israelites who had remained faithful were delivered from captivity in Babylonia.

The promises were what made Israel confident in God as deliverer. Promises are statements that affect another person's future. God was persistently the giver of promises, guaranteeing a divine participation in Israel's future. The first of these promises was given to Abraham, and it was this promise that assured the Israelites of an identity as a people. God promised: "I will bless you, and make your name great, so that you will be a blessing. I will bless those who bless you, and the one who curses you I will curse; and in you all the families of the earth shall be blessed" (Genesis 12:2–3).

God's power to keep promises was shown by giving Abraham and Sarah their first child when both were well past the usual childbearing age. To Moses, God promised a land flowing with milk and honey, a promise severely tested by a journey of forty years through the wilderness. But God's identity as the one who promises reached its culmination in the prophets. A ruler was promised from the branch of David who would be called "Wonderful Counselor, Mighty God, Everlasting Father, Prince of Peace" (Isaiah 9:6). He would be a servant who would suffer to bear the sins of many (Isaiah 53), and he would usher in the Day of the Lord, an era of peace, prosperity, and abundance. Christians have seen this promise fulfilled in God's coming among the people as Jesus and look for its fulfillment when Jesus comes again.

God gave one more thing to the Israelites that was highly prized— the law. God, the giver of gifts, gave the law as a sign of love and care. The crux of the law was given to Moses on Mount Sinai and has become known as the Ten Commandments or the Decalogue. But the Ten Commandments are just a small part of the laws that covered every aspect of Israel's daily life and cultic celebration. Giving the law was an act of love on God's part because it showed the Israelites how to live as their maker intended. No longer would they have to struggle by trial and error to figure out the lifestyle best for them. They would have a pattern to follow, clear commands for them to obey. The system in which God gave specific commands to specific people for specific situations was replaced by a law for all.

In terms of self-disclosure, the law tells us that its giver, God, has a moral quality. Throughout the Bible, writers spoke of God's holiness. God is without moral flaw. In worship, Christians sing the *Sanctus*, "Holy, holy, holy, Lord God of power and might," a song Isaiah heard the angels sing to one another before God. Whatever God wills is good and holy. Holiness also sets God apart. "The first definition of holy, then is that which is separate, mysterious, not to be touched or approached by ordinary [people].... [T]he underlying idea of holiness is . . . separation."[7] It is God's holiness revealed in the giving of the law that, when not matched by a comparable holiness on the part of God's people, mandates a fracture in that relationship.

God, the giver, who is called Father, revealed himself in activity as creator, deliverer, promise-maker and law-giver. All these revelations of self, all these activities of God, took place in history:

> Christianity among the religions seems to be the only one that takes history seriously, for it assumes that the knowledge of God is associated with events that really happened in human life.... Real events and traditions are interpreted in such a way as to reveal the nature of God and [humanity].[8]

God, the Holy Spirit

In the same way that Jesus made claims about the "Father" that gave clues to God under that name, he made promises to his disciples about the "Spirit" that would come to take his place and empower their ministries. Thus God, the giver, is revealed as the Holy Spirit as well.

Now the Holy Spirit is spoken of by Christians as a way of describing divine activity in their lives. God is the giver, but we don't take gifts from just anyone. There may be many gifts under the Christmas tree, but I may not know which one, if any, is for me. The giver has a hand in making us accept the gift and open it for ourselves. That is the activity of the Holy Spirit.

The Holy Spirit gives insight, draws people to the gospel, makes hearers understand that the gospel story is their story. Luther put it well in his explanation of the Third Article of the Apostles' Creed:

> I believe that I cannot by my own understanding or effort believe in Jesus Christ my Lord, or come to him. But the Holy Spirit has called me through the Gospel, enlightened me with his gifts, and sanctified and kept me in true faith. In the same way he calls, gathers, enlightens, and sanctifies the whole Christian church on earth, and keeps it united with Jesus Christ in the one true faith.[9]

Some prefer to see the Holy Spirit as God at work in the world today. Surely, the work of the Spirit is that of creating faith and good work in the believer and drawing believers together into a fellowship. It is the Spirit who assures us we are forgiven of our sins. Yet not just the Spirit is at work today. God's work of creation continues, and people are drawn to the living Christ today, even as the living Christ intercedes on our behalf with the Creator. Yet when we talk about having received the gift God gives, the Holy Spirit is usually given the credit.

The gender of God

I have tried to avoid using any personal pronouns when referring to God or the Holy Spirit. I have done this to minimize "God, he" talk. Yet at a time when an awareness of the effects of language on gender identity has been heightened, some comment is necessary about the predominantly masculine names by which God, the giver, has been described.

It is clear that the biblical writers used some figures of speech that would make "God the Mother" an appropriate label. In Isaiah 66:13, for example, we read, "As a mother comforts her child, so I will comfort you." Jesus used maternal imagery in referring to his own actions. "How often have I desired to gather your children together as a hen gathers her brood under her wings, and you were not willing!" (Matthew 23:37). Yet Christianity is a historical religion with a God who acts in history. As such there is great danger in rewriting the texts every time historical advances would modify the language. I resist translations that eliminate references to the three-storied universe that was part of accepted cosmology prior to Galileo. I oppose translating the demon possession of the Gospels into a form of mental illness known today, although I believe that would be scientifically accurate in some cases. As long as the focus for Christian faith is in first-century Palestine, then the usage of that day should be accepted—and then interpreted in light of what we know now. Jesus happened to be a man and therefore a son. To retranslate the documents of the Bible so as always to refer to him as Child is to blur the historicity.

Similarly, to change God the Father into God the Parent not only dehistoricizes the documents, but moves the language to another level of abstraction. As a historical faith, Christianity has used the language of historical narrative and personal experience. Our English usage does not permit "Parent" to be employed in the vocative, nor does that suggest any of the immediacy and intimacy of "Father" or "Mother."

Clearly we are in a transitional period regarding gender-related language. My preference is that, as the issue continues to be discussed, the community of faith ultimately should make the decision.

In the case of the Holy Spirit, the possibilities are wider, not because of changes in the culture, but because of ambiguities in the original text. The word translated "Spirit" from the Greek is grammatically neuter. But the Holy Spirit is personal, as are God and Jesus. If we refer to the Spirit as "it," that personal dimension is lost. The tendency to think of "her" as an object is enhanced. So, in a time of masculine dominance, "he" became the pronoun.

But the word for "Spirit" in Hebrew is feminine. Furthermore, if we look at the activities of the Spirit—guiding, comforting, teaching, and inspiring—and relate them to a gender in our society, they might be considered feminine qualities. So a good case can be made for the reference to the Holy Spirit as "she." This would then be one step in assuring that we do not attribute only maleness to God, or in a positive sense, assure that God's feminine dimension is not overlooked.

The Holy Trinity

Thus far, it appears that we have three givers instead of one. Yet Christianity insists that it is continuous with its Jewish roots in being radically monotheistic. This three-in-one nature of God is described in the doctrine of the Holy Trinity.

The doctrine of the Holy Trinity does not solve the problem as neatly as we would like. British writer Dorothy Sayers, writing answers she thought the typical Christian would give to questions of doctrine, had this response to the question "What is the doctrine of the Trinity?": "The Father incomprehensible, the Son incomprehensible, the whole thing incomprehensible. Something put in by theologians to make it more difficult—nothing to do with daily life or ethics."[10]

The doctrine of the Trinity was developed to try to explain the language of religious experience reflected in the Bible. In the book of Matthew, Jesus told his disciples to baptize "in the name of the Father and of the Son and of the Holy Spirit" (Matthew 28:19). Paul's closing benediction in the second letter to the Corinthians is well known because of its use in Christian worship: "The grace of the Lord Jesus Christ, the love of God, and the communion of the Holy Spirit be with all of you" (2 Corinthians 13:13). At Jesus' baptism, a voice from heaven was heard saying, "This is my Son, the Beloved, with whom I am well pleased." And a dove (traditionally symbolizing the Holy Spirit) descended (Matthew 3:16–17). In Colossians, Jesus was declared to be the one by whom all things were created. Yet in Genesis 1, God was the creator, and the Spirit brooded over the waters.

C. S. Lewis suggested an analogy that indicates why it is necessary to try to formulate these experiences into a doctrine if the church is to grow:

> If [people have] once looked at the Atlantic Ocean from the beach and then go and look at a map of the Atlantic, they also will be turning from something real to something less real: turning from real waves to a bit of coloured paper. But here comes the point. The map is admittedly only coloured paper, but there are two things you have to remember about it. In the first place, it is based on what hundreds of thousands of people have found out by sailing the real Atlantic.... In the second place, if you want to go anywhere, the map is absolutely necessary.[11]

So it is with doctrine. Individual religious experience may have some immediate power, but doctrines place that experience in the context of hundreds of other similar experiences and provide a guide to those without that experience.

In the Athanasian Creed the doctrine is stated this way: "We worship one God in three persons and three persons in one God without confusing the persons or dividing the substance."[12] The word *person* is used in this formula in a different way from our common usage today. It does not convey the sense of an individual center of self-consciousness. Rather the Latin term *persona* "was used in drama to designate the mask worn by players as they assumed the role of different characters."[13] Yet the notion that the three persons of the Trinity are three different ways in which God is revealed to us has been condemned as heretical.

Clearly we are left with a mystery. But mysteries are less puzzling if they do not appear unreasonable. Some analogies are often helpful to suggest this reasonableness.

A book for children called *3 in 1* compared the Trinity to an apple.[14] The apple has a peel, flesh, and a core. The peel, the flesh, and the core are each apple. Yet they are not three apples, but one. God is Father, Son, and Holy Spirit. Each is God, yet they are not three Gods, but one God. In the apple, the peel protects, lots of things are made from the flesh, and the core has seeds that produce new apples. With God, the Father is our protector. God, the Son, makes it possible for others to become sons and daughters of God. The Spirit makes faith in God grow. There is one apple and one God. (This analogy falls short in that in the Trinity anything one person does, so do the others. All three persons of the Trinity were active in creation, for example.)

With C. S. Lewis the analogy is a bit more sophisticated. We live in a three-dimensional world, he said, but if we use only one dimension, we can draw only straight lines. If we use two, we can draw a square, using four straight lines. If we use three dimensions, we can build a cube with six squares. If we move to the more complicated levels, we do not leave behind what we had in the simpler levels, but combine them in new ways, ways we could not imagine if we knew only the simpler levels.

Applied to the Trinity, the analogy works like this: Assume our human level is the one in which two persons are two separate beings, just as two squares are separate figures in a two-dimensional world. On the divine level there is a being who has three persons while remaining one being, just as a cube has six squares while remaining one cube. We cannot conceive of any being like that, but we could not imagine a cube if we were part of two-dimensional space. The Trinity becomes suprapersonal, the kind of being appropriate for the divine dimension.[15]

For a third analogy think of some creative work. A cantata by Bach first existed in the mind of the composer, where it lived its own life. Then it became incarnate in the score on paper and in the sounds produced by the orchestra and choir. Then it became a spirit so that we can talk about it and share what it meant with one another. It is the same piece of music, but it has different forms, different manifestations of itself that are each independently comprehensible but nonetheless one.

Still all analogies are approximate. Another way of gaining insight into the Trinity is to see its activity in our lives. We kneel to say our prayers, to get in touch with God. We know that it is God the Spirit who prompts us to pray and gives us motivation. We know our prayers are heard, because they are offered in the name of Jesus who intercedes for us, and we count upon the Father to hear and answer our prayers. In prayer, we are experiencing the kind of reality the doctrine of the Trinity has been developed to explain.

God, the giver, reveals God to us as the Father, the Son, and the Holy Spirit. God is revealed as creative, as incarnate, and as the enabler of faith. What we know of God, the giver, we know because of God's acts in the history of Israel and in our own history. What we do know makes us wonder about all that we do not know. Our knowledge of God is like a man standing on the beach at the edge of the Atlantic Ocean. The little portion of the coastline that touches that beach, he knows. It is real. But beyond it are incalculable miles of shoreline and ocean that he can never know intimately and about which he can only surmise. These two things he knows about, the ocean and God. The portion that touches him is real. Beyond that is new territory to be explored and ultimately to make him bend in awe.[16]

– 2 –

The Receiver

"So God created humankind in his image, in the image of God he created them" (Genesis 1:27).

"All have sinned and fall short of the glory of God" (Romans 3:23).

While it may be "more blessed to give than to receive," there is no gift-giving if there is not someone to receive the gift. Therein is the dilemma for God and the rationale for the creation of the world, and particularly of humankind. James Weldon Johnson caught that notion when he opened his poem "Creation" with the lines, "And God stepped out in space, and [God] looked around and said, 'I'm lonely, I'll make me a world.'"[1]

What was the world like that the Giver created? We need to know, for humanity is part of that created order.

First, the world was created out of nothing. We know nothing about what existed before, but we do believe, as Luther said in his meaning of the First Article of the Apostles' Creed, that God "created me and all that exists." God and creation are different orders of reality. Creation is contingent upon God and not vice versa.

This eliminates two other popular forms of belief about creation. One is pantheism—that God is a part of everything in the world. Those who worship nature fall into this category. After looking at a sunset or walking through the woods on a spring morning and being exhilarated by the experience, people often feel they have been in touch with God. Perhaps they have, but the sunset or the walk are to God like a favorite sweater or apple pie are to the mother or father who made them. They are signs, sources of recollection, but not the maker himself or herself. Christians are not pantheists.

Nor are Christians dualists. All that exists was created and continues to be created by God. Rational people find this hard to believe with the evil that is in the world—cancer, earthquakes, tyrants, and for some, demons. Christians do not deny that such evil is present, but they contend that it is a result of perversion occurring in things that God created rather than to a second agent equal in status to God.

C. S. Lewis made a strong argument against dualism. He contended that if dualism is true, the evil power must be a being who likes evil for its own sake. In reality though, we have no experience of anyone liking evil just because it is evil. All that is evil is really good things perverted, and none can be understood except in relation to the good. Evil cannot supply itself with good impulses or things to pervert. It must be getting them from the good power. If that is the case, then evil is not independent, but part of the good power's world. Thus evil is a parasite, not an original thing. All the things that enable a bad person to be effectively bad are in themselves good things—resolution, cleverness, good looks, existence itself.[2] Thus, dualism will not logically hold together.

In addition to affirming that all creation is contingent on God, the fact that God created it makes all of it good. In the Genesis account of creation, at the end of each day God saw that what had been made was good. If that is the case and God calls the material world good, so should Christians. Christians, then, are able to delight in a gourmet meal by candlelight or the aroma of new-mown hay, abandon themselves to the ecstasy of a sexual climax, and laugh and play in a mountain lake, because the things of life are part of what God made and are called good. Any kind of abstinence motivated by a belief that the things of the world are dirty or corrupting in themselves is false.

Both contingency and goodness apply to the crown of creation, the human being, the one God made to receive all the gifts. But for the human being these two qualities are not sufficient descriptions. Few questions are as fundamental in life as "Who am I?" or "What does it mean to be human?"

Modern fiction is preoccupied with the tales of those who have failed to answer those questions wisely. In Arthur Miller's famous play

Death of a Salesman, the central character, Willy Loman, kills himself. But the story is tragic not because of his death, but because both his life and his death were based on an illusion. He had lost contact with reality and depended instead on fantasies of himself as a first-rate salesman, and of his sons achieving success on the basis of strength, good looks, and personality. This requiem is said by one of his sons: "He never knew who he was."[3]

Where then does the answer to who we are come from? When we looked at who God is, we began with Jesus who is "a window up to God and a mirror up to humanity." Christians confess not just that Jesus is true God, but also that he is truly human. If he is God's way of showing us what deity is like, he is also God's way of showing us what true humanity is like.

Jesus showed that to be human is to be different from God in that we are limited by space and time. Jesus lived for a thirty-three-year period, traveled only where he could get on foot, and had the worldview, dress, and eating habits of that culture and that period in history. Even the Apostles' Creed dated him in history as suffering under Pontius Pilate.

Second, Jesus was truly human in that he responded to others and to situations emotionally. When "he saw the crowds, he had compassion for them, because they were harassed and helpless, like sheep without a shepherd" (Matthew 9:36). He wept at the death of his good friend Lazarus. He was angry at the moneychangers in the temple and sometimes at Peter for his brashness. He became fatigued and went off to sleep and pray. To be human, then, is to be involved with others and to respond to them.

Third, Jesus had a sense of self-transcendence. Three times he predicted the future for himself, knowing he had a mission to accomplish. He was able to stick to a purpose in his life. Think how easy it would have been for him to spend his whole time healing all those who came to him. He had a sense of history. He gained his identity and framed his message by references to the story of the people of Israel. Humans are distinct from the rest of creation in that they have this ability to transcend the moment and write their own story.

Jesus submitted his freedom to the will of the Father on every occasion. Jesus said straight out that he came not to do his own will, but the will of the one who sent him (John 6:38). In the Garden of Gethsemane he struggled to do God's will, wanting very much to find a way to avoid crucifixion. Yet, in the end, he said, "My Father, if it is possible, let this cup pass from me; yet not what I want but what you want" (Matthew 26:39).

To do the will of God perfectly is to be free from sin. That is exactly the claim made by the apostles about Jesus. Peter said, "'He committed no sin, and no deceit was found in his mouth.' When he was abused, he did not return abuse; when he suffered, he did not threaten; but he entrusted himself to the one who judges justly" (1 Peter 2:22–23). Speaking of Christ as our high priest, the author of the letter to the Hebrews wrote, "For we do not have a high priest who is unable to sympathize with our weaknesses, but we have one who in every respect has been tested as we are, yet without sin" (Hebrews 4:15). Ideal humanity then, as revealed in Jesus, is humanity that is perfectly in accord with the will of God.

Finally, Jesus showed true humanity in the way he loved and cared for others. At no time do we get the sense in Jesus' life that he used his charisma with a crowd or his power to please himself. Always his life was given to help others, through teaching, through healing, through advocating on behalf of the poor or outcasts, and finally through dying a death he didn't deserve. When we look for the model life, we can find no better.

Jesus, true God and true humanity

While the discussion of the Trinity gave some insight as to how Christians dealt with the divinity of Jesus, an earlier problem was how to understand Jesus as true God and true human at the same time. Historically, some explanation had to be offered for what Jaroslav Pelikan calls the inevitable tendency of the early Christians to refer to Jesus as Lord.[4] The result is the two-nature Christology. Article III of the Augsburg Confession expressed that doctrine: "God the Son, became man, born of the virgin Mary, and that the two natures, divine and human, are so inseparably united in one person that there is one true Christ, true God and true [human]."[5]

For Luther that was a sensible statement and the only rational way to understand the Bible. He would say that many verses (as in John 11) talk of Jesus as if he were human. Many others speak of him as if he were God. Thus he must be both. For example, on the human side,

Jesus waited two days before going to Bethany (v. 6); he was time-constrained again (v. 30); he had compassion (v. 33); he wept (v. 35). On the divine side, he claimed to be able to keep people who believe in him from dying (v. 25); he was declared the Messiah, the Son of God, by Martha (v. 27); he said the Father sent him (v. 42); and he raised Lazarus (v. 44). The stories of Jesus, Luther contended, could be divided in this way.

Christians before Luther had not been so easily content. Today's accepted doctrine is best understood by seeing what the church has rejected. On the one hand, it has been proposed that Jesus was a god-like human, or that he was a human being "adopted by God" for a particular purpose at his baptism, transfiguration, and resurrection. Passages such as Revelation 13:8; Colossians 1:15; and Philippians 2:5–8, which talk of the preexistent Christ, led the church to reject this formulation. Yet Jesus, the Godlike human, is implicit in the Christology of such contemporary writers as D. H. Lawrence and Nickos Kazantzakis, and it is closest to the Unitarian position.

On the other hand, Jesus could be a humanlike God. This theory was advanced by Nestorius and called Docetism. Jesus seemed to be a human who wore his humanness as a shawl. Yet, as will be explained below, such a figure could not accomplish the salvation of humanity.

The third alternative, a position midway between the two others, proposed that Jesus was a species all his own. For Eutychus the two natures were mixed together. For Arius he was in between deity and humanity. But this, too, was rejected by the church in favor of the two natures in one person, not mixed, not divisible, and not separated that came from the Councils of Chalcedon and Nicea. Characteristically, the church leaders did not say how this could be—but described the reality as they perceived God gave it.

From Jesus' life and example we learn that true humanity, the receiver of what God gives, is (1) limited by time and space, (2) responsive to others, (3) self-transcendent, (4) submissive of his or her freedom to the will of the Father, and (5) loving and caring for others. The other source about what it means to be human is the creation narrative itself. There the phrase "in the image of God" is used to describe human creation that is different from all other creation. While there is no agreement as to exactly what the image of God is, the last three of the characteristics gleaned from the examination of Jesus have all been possibilities.

But linguistically, the Hebrew words for image were used to

> designate the images the emperor might set up in lands which he ruled indicating he was lord over that area. Likewise, human beings bear God's image as they stand upon the earth, indicating they are rulers over creation yet always responsible to God.... Rather than specifying a characteristic that constitutes the image of God in a person, it is therefore more in line with the biblical witness to regard persons in their totality as reflecting who and what God is.[6]

God created human personality in such a way that communication between God and that personality is possible. There must be some point of correspondence between God, the giver, and human beings, the receivers, so that transactions can occur. The point of creation was love—the expression of God's loving nature through the creation of something that could love God in return. That potentiality is what the image of God provides.

Yet it is perfectly obvious that the whole story has not yet been told. Human beings, as we observe them, do not fit the definition we have offered. We wish they did, but common sense indicates they do not. Human beings have gone wrong in that, unlike Jesus, they have not used their freedom to do God's will. Rather, they have used it to find a way to be self-sufficient. That wrong use of freedom is what Christians call sin. The manifestations of this sin in the Bible are numerous.

Beginning with the notion that sin is some marring of the image of God in which humans are created, D. T. Niles contended that

> it is not the image of God on a coin that the image of God resembles. That image is part of the coin and cannot be separated from it. Even if the king dies, the image remains on the coin. But there is another kind of image. On a still, cloudless night we may see the image of the moon on the water of a lake. So long as the water is unruffled by the wind and the moon not covered by a cloud, the image will shine clear and beautiful. But if a cloud comes between the moon and the earth, the image will disappear; or if the water is ruffled by the wind, the image will be scattered and distorted. Thus the image of the moon on the water does not belong to the water the same way the image of the king on the coin belongs to the coin. The image depends upon a certain relationship between the moon and the water. The image of God in humanity is more like the image in the water than on the coin.[7]

Its presence depends upon a right relationship between God and people. When that relationship is disturbed, the image is distorted.

Emil Brunner provided an alternate illustration:

> Two men board a train. One of them perhaps does something sensible, the other something stupid, upon entering the coach. But as they look out, both notice they have taken the wrong train and are going in the wrong direction. That one man was reasonable and the other stupid is a difference between these two men; it is a difference, however, which has no significance in relation to the fact that both, whatever their individual differences, are going in the wrong direction! That is what the Bible means by the word sin; the total perverse direction of our life, the tendency away from God.[8]

C. S. Lewis took this travel image and expanded on it:

> There are two ways in which the human machine goes wrong. One is when human individuals drift apart from one another or else collide with one another and do one another damage by cheating or bullying. The other is when things go wrong inside the individual—when the different parts of him [or her]... either drift apart or interfere with one another. You can get the plain idea if you think of us as a fleet of ships sailing in formation. The voyage will be a success only, in the first place, if the ships do not collide and get in one another's way; and, secondly, if each ship is seaworthy and her engines in good order.... But there is one thing we have not yet taken into account. We have not asked where the fleet is trying to get to.... However well the fleet sailed, its voyage would be a failure if it were meant to reach New York and actually arrived at Calcutta.[9]

There are three different manifestations of sin then: (1) that which results from the lack of fair play between individuals; (2) that which involves the disintegration of things inside the individual; and (3) that which has to do with the general purpose of human life as a whole.

The fundamental nature of human sin has to do with this wrong direction in life. It stems from lack of belief that God is the giver of life and ultimately is in charge and control of it. Those not focusing upon God usually place themselves at the center of the universe. Thus self-centeredness is the common manifestation of unbelief. Luther referred to this as being curved in upon oneself.

Feodor Dostoyevsky is probably the novelist who most graphically explored the depth and consequence of human sin. In *Crime and Punishment*, for example, Raskolnikov sinned in a way that powerfully illustrated this self-centeredness. He murdered a pawnbroker because he was convinced that he, a brilliant student, would make a greater contribution to society than this worthless old woman. Jaroslav Pelikan analyzed that deed:

The murder of the old pawnbroker was a sin, but not merely because it was a breach of conventional morality. This made it a crime, not a sin. Raskolnikov's sin was brought on by his egocentricity, his assumption that his position in the universe was so important that he could suspend the existence of another person to advance his own ends.... Sin, therefore, was not the violation of some precept or prohibition, it was the assumption: I am God.[10]

Up to this point we have discussed sin primarily in personal terms, the individual turned in on himself or herself. Yet it is clear from the Old Testament prophets that sin was a societal issue as well, and that people bear the consequences of institutional failure whether they "feel" them or not. Amos railed against the nation's iniquities:

For three transgressions of Israel,
and for four, I will not revoke the punishment;
because they sell the righteous for silver,
and the needy for a pair of sandals—
they who trample the head of the poor into the dust of the earth,
and push the afflicted out of the way;
father and son go in to the same girl,
so that my holy name is profaned;
they lay themselves down beside every altar
on garments taken in pledge;
and in the house of their God they drink
wine bought with fines they imposed (Amos 2:6–8).

It is not hard to apply these same indictments to the United States in relationship to the developing countries of the Third World. Ron Sider asked:

Are housing, education and job opportunities in our area inferior for people not of our own skin colour, for instance? Why do fifty percent of the children in Central America die of starvation or malnutrition by the age of five—at the same time that fifty percent of the good land in Central America is used to grow export crops for affluent North Americans and Europeans? We need to look at the present plight of minorities and of the poor to ask to what extent their problems are due to sin in the system.[11]

Nuclear arms, ecology, the subjugation of women, racism, and the national budget are areas where self-interest of a nation or individuals may predominate over God's will. In each there are evidences of sin. While it is customary for people to deny their culpability because they are not directly responsible for the policy in any one area, Christianity does not permit such an easy out. There are sins of *commission*, to be sure, but we are responsible for what we fail to do as well. These are sins of *omission*. As citizens in a democratic country, we can work to bring change in our institutions and society for the sake of justice, but most of the time we don't. In the Brief Order for Confession and Forgiveness, we confess that "we have sinned against you in thought, word and deed, by what we have done and what we have left undone."[12] That confession echoes Paul's words, "For I do not do the good I want, but the evil I do not want is what I do" (Romans 7:19).

The tragic fact about human life is not just that sin occurred, but that it is inevitable. Because of the fall (the "original sin"), all people inevitably sin. The Augsburg Confession stated this without qualification: "Our churches also teach that since the fall of Adam, all [people] who are propagated according to nature are born in sin. That is to say, they are without the fear of God, are without trust in God, and are concupiscent." The contention here is that in the story of Adam and Eve the origin of sin and its inevitability are explained.

Interpretations of that story are varied. Luther understood Genesis 3 as history. Our original parents, those from whom all the human race descended, used their free will after being tempted by the serpent and disobeyed the one command God had given them—not to eat of the tree of the knowledge of good and evil. Their disobedience destroyed the perfection of creation and the unclouded relationship between them and God. Once perfection had been destroyed, it could not be restored. Our first parents were punished for their disobedience by banishment from the garden, by pain in childbirth, by the need to toil to survive, and by death.

However, one does not have to read the story historically to understand original sin. The Adam and Eve account may be the account of everyone, giving us a clue to the dark or rebellious side of character, a revelation of the fact that we choose to disobey as well. Or it may be the story of the collective human race personified in these people. The message remains. Sinfulness is now a part of being human.

Those who quarrel with this notion are by and large rugged individualists. They believe they are who they are because of what they have done, and they receive rewards and punishments on that basis alone. Yet it is clear both psychologically and biblically that we take some of the credit and blame for characteristics of groups to which we belong.

Biblically, the human race is regarded as a unit, as is the nation of Israel and its postresurrection equivalent, the Christian church. Both the blessings and curses of belonging to these groups are shared by everyone in them. To be part of humanity is to share in its sinfulness. The phrase "the iniquity of the parents will be visited on the children to the third and fourth generation" is repeated often in the Old Testament (see, for example, Exodus 20:5; 34:7; Numbers 14:18; Deuteronomy 5:9). Such a statement seems unfair. Yet in the solidarity of the human race there are consequences—for good and for ill.

Still, some people do not perceive themselves as sinners. God has made certain that we do not have to come to the awareness that we are sinners on our own. The law, especially the Ten Commandments, was given to Israel both as a gift to help them live happily and also as a measuring stick against which they could evaluate their lives. Paul insisted that any honest evaluation will find the person coming up wanting. "'No human being,'" Paul wrote, "'will be justified in his sight' by deeds prescribed by the law, for through the law comes the knowledge of sin" (Romans 3:20).

The law is not just an Old Testament phenomenon. Jesus' command, "Be perfect, therefore, as your heavenly Father is perfect" (Matthew 5:48), is stricter than anything we might find in the Old Testament. In the Sermon on the Mount, Jesus made the law more stringent than did other Jews of his time. "You have heard it said of old," he said, "but I say…" He included even looking at a woman lustfully under the command, "Thou shalt not commit adultery," and anger against another as a form of "Thou shall not kill." Jesus summarized the law, "'You shall love the Lord your God with all your heart, and with all your soul, and with all your mind.' This is the greatest and first commandment. And a second is like it: You shall love your neighbor as yourself. On these two commandments hang all the law and the prophets" (Matthew 22:37–40). While this summary adds nothing to the Old Testament witness, neither have those two commands been perfectly obeyed.

Contrary to the way people use the law—to determine how to behave and thereby win God's favor—the law teaches Christians how sinful we are (see Galatians 3:24). We can take no pride in how much of the law we have kept, but only ask for mercy and confess our failure in falling short.

The fact that there is a law by which God judges humanity is probably the most countercultural teaching of the faith. Christianity asserts that this law comes from God. It is absolute. Whether any particular person argues with it or not, everyone will be held accountable to it (and found wanting). Relativism is the prevailing philosophy practiced in our time. People can decide what is right and wrong, what to believe and not believe for themselves. The operating principle for most people's lives is that it doesn't matter what you believe as long as it is helpful to you and you are sincere. Morals are a matter of taste. Christians, on the other hand, take the stance that there is a moral law and a God. Furthermore, to say this is to be making statements about the nature of reality that are as true or false as a statement like, "It's raining outside." That there is an absolute moral law may be more difficult—or even impossible—to verify, but if there is, one stands to be judged by the law as surely as one stands to get wet from the rain.

If all humanity has sinned and fallen short of the glory of God, what are the consequences? Paul set forth the answer as clearly as one would hope to have it: "For the wages of sin is death," (Romans 6:23). What Paul was talking about is literal physical death, the cessation of existence. Presumably, if humanity had not sinned, no one would die. Death can also be perceived as separation from God, who is the epitome of life itself. Paul certainly understood that as well. The writer of Genesis 3 who wrote, "You are dust, and to dust you shall return," conveyed that the consequence of sin from the very beginning is death.

Death has forms we experience prior to physical cessation of life. *Guilt* is one. Guilt is the death of self-worth. As much as psychologists following Freud have done to try to rid us of that concept, most people do have guilty consciences. Theologian Paul Tillich put it this way:

> We do not like words such as "sin" and "punishment." They seem to us old-fashioned, barbaric and invalid in the light of modern psychology. But whenever I have met exiles of high moral standards and insight, I have discovered that they feel responsible for what has happened within their own countries. And often I have met citizens of democratic countries who have expressed a feeling of guilt for the situation of the world today. They were right, and the exiles were right; they are responsible, as are you and I. Whether or not we call it sin, whether or not we call it punishment, we are beaten by the consequences of our own failures. That is the order of history.[13]

That sense of responsibility is the source of guilt.

Modern literature has countless examples of people struggling with guilt, often by denial. In Franz Kafka's *The Trial*, the central figure was under arrest for a crime he didn't know, by a court he couldn't describe. But he wandered into a cathedral and met a priest who summarized his position:

> "You are an accused man," said the priest in a very low voice. "Yes," said K., "so I have been informed." . . . "Do you know that your case is going badly?" asked the priest. "I have had that idea myself," said K. "I've done what I could, but without any success so far." . . . "How do you think it will end?" asked the priest. "At first I thought it must turn out well," said K., "but now I frequently have my doubts. I don't know how it will end. Do you?" "No," said the priest, "but I fear it will end badly. You are held to be guilty. Your case will perhaps never get beyond a lower court. Your guilt is supposed, for the present at least, to have been proved." "But I am not guilty," said K. "It's a misunderstanding. And if it comes to that, how can [anyone] be called guilty? We are all simply [human] here, one as much as the other." "That is true," said the priest, "but that is how all guilty [people] talk."[14]

The ramifications of this denial are serious and count for a major part of the boredom of our time. Herbert Mowrer said:

> So long as [people live] under the shadow of real, unacknowledged and unexpiated guilt, [they] . . . will continue to hate [themselves] and to suffer the inevitable consequences of self-hatred. But the moment [they] . . . begin to accept [their] guilt and . . . sinfulness, the possibility of radical reformation opens up, and . . . a new freedom of self-respect and peace.[15]

A second form of death that is a consequence of sin is *despair,* the death of hope. One despairs when the power for good and change in life seems less strong than the power of evil. This despair is a denial of the almightiness of God. Those who believe in a God who acts in history cannot remain in despair.

Arthur Miller is one contemporary writer who wrote of the experience of despair:

> When you're young you prove how brave you are, how smart; then, what a good lover; then a good father; finally, how wise or powerful or what the hell ever. But underlying it all, I see now, there is a presumption. That I was moving on an upward path towards some elevation, where—God knows what—I would be justified or even condemned— a verdict anyway. I think now that my disaster really began when I looked up one day—and the bench was empty. No judge in sight. And all that remained was the endless argument with oneself—this pointless litigation of existence before an empty bench. Which, of course, is another way of saying—despair.[16]

Despair is an increasingly prevalent response to life, not so much generated by personal failure, but by the overwhelming prospects of nuclear and ecological holocausts. Students who have not succeeded in blocking out thoughts of the future often have trouble generating enthusiasm for it because their very existence in it seems tenuous.

Similar kinds of examples could be cited for *rebellion*, the death of authority; *alienation*, the death of love; or *indulgence*, the death of meaning. But the point has been made. The consequence of sin is not just death in a juridical sense in relation to God. Death is an experienced reality that takes different forms for different people. Add to this the social forms of death—war, oppression, disease, corruption, exploitation—and it is easy to see why for Christians sin is at the heart of our existence. It is the basis, the root explanation, for all that we dislike in ourselves, in others and in the world. Its manifestations are severe. There is no easy remedy.

The human being, the receiver of God's gift, cannot be fully understood by affirming two seemingly contradictory statements. (In theology, contradictory statements are called paradoxes or dialectics and serve to illustrate that our reason is not yet adequate to encompass our experience.) On the one hand, humans are part of God's good creation, created in God's own image. On the other, they are thoroughly and inevitably sinful. Russian novelist Aleksandr Solzhenitsyn captured that thought well:

> If only it were all so simple! If only there were evil people somewhere insidiously committing evil deeds, and it were necessary only to separate them from the rest of us and destroy them. But the line dividing good and evil cuts through the heart of every human being. And who is willing to destroy a piece of [one's] own heart?
>
> During the life of any heart this line keeps changing place; sometimes it is squeezed one way by exuberant evil and sometimes it shifts to allow enough space for good to flourish. One and the same human being is, at various ages, under various circumstances, a totally different human being: at times [one] is close to being a devil, at times to sainthood. But [one's] name doesn't change, and to that name we ascribe the whole lot, good and evil. . . .
>
> From good to evil is one quaver, says the proverb.
> And correspondingly, from evil to good.[17]

~ 3 ~

The Gift

"For the wages of sin is death, but the free gift of God is eternal life in Christ Jesus our Lord" (Romans 6:23).

God, the giver, found humans, the receivers, alienated from God and subject to the penalty for sin, which is death. However much they may have wanted to, there was no way for them to restore their relationship to God. So God took the initiative and gave to humans the gift they needed most: salvation, a restored relationship to their creator and deliverance from death. God had given gifts before—the world, the law, deliverance from oppression, even Jesus, God's only Son. But the gift beyond all others was salvation.

Now, in the New Testament, salvation, means health and safety and deliverance from all the enemies of that health and safety.[1] God saves. The witness of the New Testament is that this gift is given through the death of Jesus Christ. The cross accomplished all that was necessary for all people to receive salvation.

Models of the Atonement

The Christian church has more than one way to explain how the death on the cross accomplished this. No single doctrine of atonement (at-one-ment) is proposed and accepted as authoritative. Rather, at different times in history, different models have seemed to make the most sense. Models are just that. They are means, never fully accurate in themselves, by which a given phenomenon can be understood.

In physics the wave and particle theories of light are studied because each tells something about how light behaves. But if a model is not helpful, it should be discarded. The idea that Jesus' death on the cross restored our relationship to God is crucial. Efforts to explain how that occurred are expendable. What follows is an effort to incorporate most of the traditional answers to the questions of how Jesus' death accomplished salvation.

Often when New Testament writers wrote about the death of Christ, they used phrases that express purpose. It was of no interest to them that Jesus died unless that death accomplished something. From the practical point of view, *how* it accomplished something is a matter of mere curiosity. What is of concern is *what* was accomplished—what was the purpose of Jesus' death? I have singled out five Bible verses with purposive clauses that express what the church has understood Christ's death to accomplish.

Each of the five verses will be discussed in the following way. First, the "traditional" kind of bondage from which Christ's death frees the believer will be examined. Luther saw the Christian in bondage to sin, the law, the wrath of God, the devil, and death. In contemporary culture, believers do not use these words to identify their experiential reality, so I have given some contemporary expressions of the problem to help tie the older terms to realities we experience. Finally, in order to rationalize how Christ's death does free believers over the course of history, various "models of the atonement" have been proposed. These models correspond to the kind of bondage a particular thinker finds central (see chart).

In discussing the atonement we note that the knowledge of theories or facts does not produce salvation. Luther said that Christ could have died a thousand times to no avail if that death was not preached so that people understood he died *for them*. Any effort to describe the atonement must be done to help personalize the concept. Thus, the personal ramifications of each of these models is central.

Model 1: Sacrificial

"So Christ, having been offered once to bear the sins of many, will appear a second time, not to deal with sin, but to save those who are eagerly waiting for him" (Hebrews 9:28).

The cross of Christ, first and foremost, solved the problem of human sin. Sin breaks the relationship with God and must be dealt with if that relationship is to be restored. The problem of sin, as we have seen, was not new with the advent of Jesus. The nation of Israel had a clear sense of transgression. Thus God had provided a means whereby their sins could be erased. On the Day of Atonement, animals were sacrificed and their blood offered for the sins of the people by the high priest. The ritual was elaborate, and the day was a high point in the life of the people. On that day a goat was selected to be the "scapegoat." By laying on of hands, the sins of the people were laid on a goat that bore them away into the wilderness where it was killed or died.

Purpose clause	Traditional bondage (Luther)	Contemporary expression of problem	Model of the atonement
"bear the sins of many" (Hebrews 9:28)	sin	indulgence	sacrificial
"redeem those who were under the law, so that we might receive adoption as children" (Galatians 4:5)	law	guilt	penal
"so that in him we might become the righteousness of God" (2 Corinthians 5:21)	wrath of God	alienation	satisfaction
"so that he might be Lord of both the dead and the living" (Romans 14:9)	devil	rebellion	ransom
"redeem us from all iniquity and purify for himself a people of his own who are zealous for good deeds" (Titus 2:14)	death	apathy	moral influence

The Sacrificial Model of the atonement, which is outlined most fully in the book of Hebrews, is based on the idea that Jesus had taken the roles of both priest and victim in the sacrifice for sin. The sinlessness of Christ was compared to the blemish-free animals used for the sacrifices. The shedding of Christ's blood was significant, because "without the shedding of blood there is no forgiveness of sins" (Hebrews 9:22). The Israelite sacrifice had to be offered annually, but because Jesus was God, his sacrifice could be "once for all" (Hebrews 10:10). Thus Christians no longer make sacrifices for sin since the sufficient eternal sacrifice was made by Jesus himself.

The other Old Testament source for the idea of sacrifice is in Isaiah 53. In that chapter the suffering servant, whom Christians identify as Jesus, will bear the sins of many. "Upon him was the punishment that made us whole . . . like a lamb that is led to the slaughter" (vv. 5–7). In this model God alone takes the initiative. God provides the sacrifice that is needed to restore the relationship with humankind that sin has broken. The sacrifice is the gift, even as the new relationship is a gift.

Since "sin" is not a popular word, we could think of sin as indulgence. The manifestations of sin for which Israel repented were those wherein they had chosen to follow their own desires rather than the will of God— that is, they chose to "indulge" themselves. When Paul listed the works of the flesh as "fornication, impurity, licentiousness, idolatry, sorcery, enmities, strife, jealousy, anger, quarrels, dissensions, factions, envy, drunkenness, carousing, and things like these" (Galatians 5:19-21), he was enumerating the various kinds of passions in which humans indulge when left unchecked by God's will. These are the very sins Christ came to bear.

While the cultic sacrificial system is not part of our Western experience today, much of Christian literature is filled with imagery of this sort. The hymns that talk about being "washed in the blood" have this motif in mind. The "Lamb of God" sung just prior to Holy Communion expresses this theme. In another context, we talk of the blood of soldiers sacrificed to defend their country. Tertullian, one of the ancient church fathers, said, "The blood of the martyrs is the seed of the church,"[2] again indicating how blood shed in death can benefit others. Christ was offered once "to bear the sins of many."

Model 2: Penal

"God sent his Son . . . to redeem those who were under the law, so that we might receive adoption as children" (Galatians 4:4–5).

The theme of Paul's letters to the Galatians and Romans is that the law, which had been given as a gift from God, had now become a burden. The law persistently accuses humans of being sinful. It drives them to repentance, but it is a burden to fulfill. Yet the law stands as the symbol of God's justice, and the cross of Christ is where God's love and God's justice are reconciled. The penalty for breaking the law is paid by one who did not deserve the penalty himself. Humankind sinned. The penalty for sin is death (Romans 6:23). Jesus became human but did not sin. He voluntarily took the penalty that belonged to humanity. Because he was also God, the transaction was sufficient for all people through all time. God's justice as judge was satisfied by God's love in Christ Jesus.

The notion that God's justice should be set aside and humanity forgiven by decree, which some use as an argument against this understanding of the atonement, makes a mockery of laws that hold the universe in order. A judge who doesn't administer the penalties for crimes will ultimately convince society that the laws do not need to be obeyed. Anarchy and chaos are the results. Similarly, parents who do not restrain the destructive and antisocial behavior of their children are not praiseworthy but irresponsible. Their children infringe upon the peace and tranquility of others. In order to maintain the viability of the law, the penalty must be exacted.

A simple story illustrates this model well:

> Let us assume that there was once in a foreign country a tribe of people who were destroying the tribal existence through excessive drink. Everybody was brewing his own beverages and consuming them thirstily. Eventually no work was done and the tribe began to disintegrate. The chief finally decided something had to be done. Only a very severe punishment would stop this road to destruction. He proclaimed that the next person who brewed some of this strong drink would be punished severely—fifty lashes over the back with a bullwhip. The severity stopped the rioting. Slowly the village recovered and the tribe went back to work. And then one day there was another drunken riot. The chief tried to find out who had brewed the drink but no one would tell him. Finally he discovered that it had been his old mother who had been responsible. What was he to do? If he punished her, the old woman would not survive and he would be responsible for the execution of his own mother. If he did not punish her, he had lost the right to punish anybody else. Chaos would return and the tribe would be doomed to destruction. Well, when the hour

of judgment approached and his mother was brought before him, the chief found her guilty as charged. But instead of having her punished, he stepped from his throne and ordered the executioner to give him fifty lashes. In this way justice was preserved and his mother's life was saved.[3]

This penal theory of the atonement is also called the juridical or courtroom model because the primary concern is with satisfying God's justice and upholding the law. In a permissive society, this model does not have the ring of authenticity that it has in those societies where the rules are clear and justly and regularly enforced.

The contemporary condition this model of the atonement addresses is guilt. Guilt is a legal as well as psychological term. Against one found guilty, the charge cannot be dismissed. The sacrament of penance practiced by Roman Catholics recognizes that psychological guilt is more easily eradicated if some compensatory act is undertaken for the offense. When it is not imposed by authority, people often generate punishment on their own.

Model 3: Satisfaction

"For our sake he made him to be sin who knew no sin, so that in him we might become the righteousness of God" (2 Corinthians 5:21).

Because humans are sinners as a result of original sin, it is impossible for humans to become righteous by their own efforts. Yet God is righteous and has fellowship only with the righteous. In order to make us righteous, God gives humans an "alien righteousness which we put on like a cloak," as Luther said.

Luther made the discovery of this righteousness in his own pilgrimage with God. He had striven endlessly to do what was right. With each apparent accomplishment came a new flush of self-righteousness and pride that left him no better off than he had been before. Then he read Romans 3:28, "For we hold that a person is justified by faith apart from works prescribed by the law." Paul said that "apart from law, the righteousness of God has been disclosed . . . the righteousness of God through faith in Jesus Christ for all who believe" (Romans 3:21–22). A little later Paul wrote: "For just as by the one man's disobedience the many were made sinners, so by the one man's obedience the many will be made righteous" (Romans 5:19). Thus, by Jesus' obedience and death on the cross, righteousness comes as the gift of God to the believer.

By making us righteous God deals with the wrath human sin provokes. "For the wrath of God is revealed from heaven against all ungodliness and wickedness of those who by their wickedness suppress the truth" (Romans 1:18). To illustrate the model, Anselm of Canterbury in *Cur Deus Homo* saw Christ on the cross as satisfying God's wrath.

Gabriel Fackre summarized this model:

> Here is a locus with a passion and death that suggests the scale of agony and punishment appropriate to sin and guilt.... The death of Christ on the cross meets the divine severity and turns aside the wrath of God.... In Anselm's "satisfaction" theory, couched in the language of medieval serf-lord relationships and the penance system of the Middle Ages, the death of Christ is a beyond-the-call-of-duty act, much like the extraordinary sacrifices of saints and monks whose consequent store of heavenly merits were thought to be transferable to sinners. Thus the favor won from [God] by the merits of Christ's supererogatory sacrifice on the cross satisfies the offended honor of the Lord.[4]

To put it another way,

> God is an infinite being and any offense against him is likewise infinite. Human beings, because of their sinfulness and their infinite offense against God, owe [God] an indefinite debt. Because they are finite, human beings cannot possibly pay that debt. They therefore deserve infinite punishment. But with the crucifixion, the finite sufferings of Jesus on the cross are the infinite sufferings of God.... If you add up all the pain and suffering through the years . . . that is only a finite amount. But God's suffering, like [God's] love, is infinite and knows no limits. [God's] suffering is for the sake of others, for their benefit as well as in their place.[5]

In both making us righteous and in satisfying God's righteousness, God is again the initiator and acts through Christ to accomplish that which humans lack the ability to do. Righteousness and the appeasement of God's wrath are both gifts.

The wrath of God is not a popular concept today. However, alienation is a sociological category very much in vogue. To the extent that people feel the wrath of God (although they cannot name it as such) they are put off, alienated. To the extent that they are made righteous, they feel accepted and acceptable, and their alienation is overcome.

Model 4: Ransom

"For to this end Christ died and lived again, so that he might be Lord of both the dead and the living" (Romans 14:9).

The New Testament pictures a genuine struggle going on between God and the forces of evil. Paul talked about how "our struggle is not against enemies of blood and flesh, but against the rulers, against the authorities, against the cosmic powers of this present darkness, against the spiritual forces of evil in the heavenly places" (Ephesians 6:12). The reason humans so frequently sin is because the devil tempts them in the battle for human loyalty. That means that if the cross could bring about the defeat of the devil, Christ would in fact be Lord without rival of both the living and the dead.

Luther wrote with his usual color about how Christ can snare the devil:

> I once beheld a wolf tearing sheep. When the wolf comes into a sheepfold, he eats not any until he has killed all, and then he begins to eat, thinking to devour all. Even so it is with the devil; I have now, thinks he, taken hold on Christ, and in time I will also snap his disciples. But the devil's folly is that he sees not that he has to do with the Son of God; he knows not that in the end it will be his bane. It will come to that pass, that the devil must be afraid of a child in a cradle; for when he but hears the name of Jesus uttered in true faith, then he cannot stay. The devil would rather run through fire than stay where Christ is. . . . I often delight myself with that similitude in Job, of an angle-hook that fishers cast into the water, putting on the hook a little worm; then comes the fish and snatches at the worm, and gets therewith the hook in his jaws, and the fisher pulls him out of the water. Even so has our Lord God dealt with the devil. God has cast into the water his Son as the angle, and upon the hook has put Christ's humanity, as the worm; then comes the devil and snaps at the . . . Christ, and devours him, and therewith he bites the iron hook, that is, the godhead of Christ, which chokes him, and all his power is thereby thrown to the ground.[6]

Luther believed in the devil and forces of evil active in the world with a certainty that is hard to find today. The time is past when science must be able to analyze something for people to believe it is real. The interest in the occult, parapsychology, and spiritualism is evidence of that. But people prefer to locate evil in other people rather than in "spiritual forces in heavenly places." Fortunately, no church has made belief in the devil a required teaching. Yet in continuity with the early church, many Christians persist in asking people before baptism (or the parents and sponsors of infants), "Do you renounce all the forces of evil, the devil and all his empty promises?"[7] It appears that the more spiritually sensitive one becomes, the more one perceives evil as well as good spirits.

After the overwhelming and surprising popularity of his book, *The Screwtape Letters*, the correspondence between a senior and junior devil, C. S. Lewis was asked often, "Do you believe in the devil?" His response is worth repeating:

> Now if by "the devil" you mean a power opposite to God and, like God, self-existent from all eternity, the answer is certainly No. There is no uncreated being except God. God has no opposite. No being could attain a "perfect badness" opposite to the perfect goodness of God; for when you have taken away every kind of good thing (intelligence, will, memory, energy and existence itself) there would be [nothing] left.
>
> The proper question is whether I believe in devils. I do. That is to say, I believe in angels, and I believe that some of these, by abuse of their free will, have become enemies of God and, as a corollary, to us. These we may call devils. They do not differ in nature from good angels, but their nature is depraved. Devil is the opposite of angel only as Bad Man is the opposite of Good Man. Satan, the leader or dictator of devils, is the opposite, not of God, but of [Archangel] Michael.
>
> I believe this not in the sense that it is part of my creed, but in the sense that it is one of my opinions. My religion would not be in ruins if this opinion were shown to be false. Till that happens—and proofs of a negative are hard to come by—I shall retain it. It seems to me to explain a good many facts. It agrees with the plain sense of scripture, the tradition of Christendom, and the beliefs of most [people] at most times. And it conflicts with nothing any of the sciences has shown to be true.[8]

Given then the possibility of evil forces operating in the world against God, one model of the atonement is based upon victory over those forces through Christ's death on the cross. The theory's origin was with Ignatius. Luther revived it, and most recently Gustaf Aulén has given it new currency. The essence of the theory is that the humanity of Christ was the foil that deceived the devil, and the divinity of Christ then destroyed the devil's power and the power of all evil forces. The means was deception, but the logic of how this deception brought victory remains a mystery.

The fanfare and grandeur of some of the Reformation chorales give the militaristic and triumphal tone appropriate for this model. In Luther's "A Mighty Fortress Is Our God," for example, the ancient foe's defeat is heralded:

A mighty fortress is our God,
A sword and shield victorious.
[God] breaks the cruel oppressor's rod
And wins salvation glorious.
The old satanic foe
Has sworn to work us woe!
With craft and dreadful might
[It] arms [itself] to fight.
On earth [God] has no equal.
No strength of ours can match [its] might!
We would be lost, rejected.
But now a champion comes to fight,
Whom God [alone] elected.
You ask who this may be?
The Lord of hosts is he!
Christ Jesus, mighty Lord,
God's only Son, adored.
He holds the field victorious.[9]

It is fully consistent with Luther's understanding of the atonement that this hymn, which tells the story of the cosmic battle, should be the song by which Lutherans are known.

For those who reject the devil, the notion of rebellion is still acceptable. The devil is the personification of rebellion. Our experience of rebellion from authority, from peace and order, from the law, is a product of the evil at work in the world. Sometimes peace can be restored only with a show of might and power that is victorious. The cross was the place where the rebellion was quelled.

The problem with this understanding is that it does not fit with our experience. Evil remains very much present in the world. Some contend that it is more potent than ever before—look at the Holocaust or Hiroshima and Nagasaki. The creators of the model contend that in principle the victory is won, if not fully actualized. Christ's coming again will usher in the time when the victory is apparent everywhere. At Gettysburg, the North won the decisive battle of the Civil War, but the battles in other places continued for some time until the word reached them that further fighting was useless. So it is with the victory at Calvary.

Model 5: Moral influence

Christ . . . "who gave himself for us that he might redeem us from all iniquity and purify for himself a people of his own who are zealous for good deeds" (Titus 2:14).

In all the other models of the atonement, a transaction takes place on a cosmic scale, setting right the moral order of the universe. In this model, the crucifixion of Christ elicits a change in humans. Purity comes as humans perceive the extent of God's love and are moved by the powerful display of love on the cross to live generously themselves.

Peter Abelard is the theologian who first formulated this thread in the witness about Christ's death. The theory is labeled the "moral influence" model of the atonement. Christ's crucifixion reveals the ultimate extent to which one person can go to manifest love for others. This example elicits faith and love on the part of the believer. Death is conquered, because if humans are willing to follow the example and lay down their lives for others, death is not feared. One fears death only when it is something over which one has no control. Voluntary death does not arouse fear.

Abelard put it this way:

> But to us it seems that by this means we are justified in the blood of Christ and reconciled to God; through this particular favor manifested toward us, that [God's] Son assumed our nature and persisted even until death in instructing us both by word and example, he has very strongly drawn us to himself through love, so that, inflamed by his great benefaction of divine grace, true love now shrinks not from the endurance of anything whatsoever.[10]

In this model it does not appear that all of salvation is accomplished by Christ. The efficacy of the atonement is contingent upon the subjective response in the believer.

Yet from the personal involvement perspective, this view is superior to the others. Preaching, hymnody, devotional piety, and religious experience all find this model the most fertile for their expression. Since loving behavior has not been successfully commanded by the law, perhaps it can be evoked by Jesus' example:

When I survey the wondrous cross
On which the prince of glory died,
My richest gain I count but loss
And pour contempt on all my pride.

Were the whole realm of nature mine,
That were a tribute far too small;
Love so amazing, so divine,
Demands my soul, my life, my all![11]

Both sacraments can be understood in light of this model. In Baptism we are "buried with him by baptism into death" (Romans 6:4)—his suffering and love. In Communion we are to proclaim the Lord's death until he comes. The context clearly makes our participation in Communion a participation in the love that suffers—the kind of love for which the cross stands.

Death can be described as apathy. People feel as if nothing matters and there is no reason to care or become involved. When the gift of salvation and life has such a high cost in terms of undeserved suffering and pain, it is difficult not to care and respond. If Christ would do that for me, I must be able to do something for him and others. As it is hard to visit the camp at Dachau and remain apathetic and unmoved, so it is hard to meditate upon Christ's undeserved death and not want to make a response.

Daniel Erlander takes the cross as the central motif in his writing about the Christian faith:

> The central visual symbol in almost every Lutheran worship room is the cross, the cruel instrument of torture and death which the Roman Empire reserved for rebellious slaves, violent criminals and threatening political subversives.
>
> The symbol is central because we confess, "It is here on the cross that God meets us." Here God [is] present . . .
> - hidden in weakness
> - vulnerable
> - suffering
> - forsaken
> - dying
>
> In the abyss of despair, in the deepest darkness, God comes. In the painful reality of our mortality, our ultimate loneliness, our weakness God encounters us. As we view the cross, all of our human attempts to find [God] are exposed as illusions. We do not find God. God finds us— in our darkness, our pain, our emptiness, our loneliness, our weakness....
>
> The cross is God's embrace: God enters our darkness and embraces us with total and unconditional acceptance. Identifying

completely with the pain and sorrow of our existence, God woos us into a love relationship with [God].

The cross is God's victory. God enters our darkness and exposes and defeats the powers that reign in this world. By the death of Jesus, God liberates us from any person, thing, system or "ism" which would enslave us by demanding absolute loyalty. We are free! Free to let God be God. Free to be human.[12]

Here more profoundly than in any other model, Jesus' admonition to take up our cross daily and follow him is made clear. The cross changes people—the way they see, the way they behave, the way they develop a vision for the future, the way they evaluate their achievements. Those changes are the basis for the renewal of our relationship with God.

I believe that Christians are not required to choose among these five models. Each contributes something crucial to our understanding of the cross of Christ. Jesus' death is not a flat, single-dimensional event. As a historical event it is viewed from different perspectives. Each is helpful for a particular situation.

The verse of scripture that seems to capture something of each of the models is 1 Peter 3:18: "For Christ also suffered for sins (Model 1) once for all, the righteous for the unrighteous (Models 2 and 3), in order to bring you to God (Model 4). He was put to death in the flesh, but made alive in the spirit" (Model 5).

The Resurrection

The resurrection of Jesus Christ has been examined here as testimony and evidence of his divinity. If the gift of God is salvation, a restored relationship to God, the only guarantee we have is the resurrection. Only the "moral influence" understanding of the crucifixion remains viable if Christ was not raised from the dead. By raising Jesus, God gave testimony to the fact that the death had accomplished its purpose. The new order had begun, and Jesus was to be the first fruit of that order. In terms of victory over death, the resurrected Christ is a model of what will happen to all believers.

The Ascension

In the Apostles' Creed, Christians also profess that Jesus "ascended into heaven, and is seated on the right hand of God the Father almighty."

Many would prefer to ignore the ascension because it made Jesus appear like the first astronaut. Some are so offended that they demythologize the story to make Jesus' ascension the sign of "upward social mobility."[13] But in terms of the salvation accomplished for us by Jesus Christ, it is the sign that this work is done and effective. Karl Barth discussed the ascension under the rubric of "The Homecoming of the Son of Man"[14] and rightfully so. For even Jesus' resurrection did not provide full assurance that the victory had been won. Perhaps, like Lazarus, Jesus would die again. The ascension reveals that, as a matter of fact, all those things that hold us back from a relationship with God have been defeated. Jesus acts as a representative human at this point and shows in a real way that we have been reunited with God. Gilbert Doan put it well:

> The cosmic drama ends as a veritable open sea rescue operation. Picture a little outboard foundering on the swirling currents of a whirlpool. Picture the men aboard sick with exhaustion and the gas and oars long gone. The boat is not yet lost down the funnel, but it veers closer and closer. A rescue cutter sights the boat, but cannot reach it or make fast to it for the sea is too rough and the men too weak to catch or hold a line. So the strongest man aboard the cutter takes a coiled line over his shoulder and dives into the water. He swims to the little boat, makes one end of the line fast to a cleat, and swims the other end of the line back to the cutter, climbs aboard and makes it fast to a winch. There is still much to be done for sure, but in fact the boat has been saved.
>
> Now what good would it do for this heroic swimmer just to dive into the waves and get drowned? Or even join the men in the boat? Or even bend one end of the cleat? Or even jump out again and swim safely ashore? Enough said. He obviously has to get back to the cutter.[15]

The ascension is Jesus' return to the cutter, making the gift of salvation secure.

God, the giver, gives to human beings the gift of salvation, a restored relationship to their God. That gift has many names: reconciliation; redemption; forgiveness; wholeness; and victory over sin, death, the law, the devil, and God's wrath. How the gift is given, purchased, secured, is a matter for speculation, but the cost was very high—the death of God's only Son.

— 4 —

Response to the Gift

"Thanks be to God for his indescribable gift!" (2 Corinthians 9:15).

The almost automatic response to any gift is to say, "Thank you." It is thought rude to say nothing and leave a gift unacknowledged. But when the gift is right, there is no danger. Appreciation can overflow to the point of tears.

Our relationship with God is that kind of gift. Paul Tournier wrote, "The universal quest for gifts is nothing other than a seeking after God by whatever name we may call [God]. For only the one who has made all things and who owns all things can give them without asking anything in return except our gratitude."[1] That is all God asks.

Faith

Unlike most of the gifts we receive, there is some problem with whether God's gift gets delivered or opened. God's gift of salvation was given once and for all on Good Friday, but many do not seem to realize it is addressed to them. They may be too wrapped up in other pursuits to stop and open it. Those who "open it" are those whom we say exhibit "faith." The process of receiving the gift is the process of having faith.

When looked at carefully, faith is a much more complex phenomenon than it first seems. It is the heart of the Christian message. Most religions of the world maintain that one's salvation is contingent on behavior. Christians believe in justification (being made or accounted righteous) by faith.

A proper understanding of faith is not easily reached. Faith is not believing things to be true that are not true. Nor is faith the source of knowledge for whatever science cannot demonstrate. While faith involves knowledge, it is not fundamentally an esoteric source of wisdom.

Faith involves three things. First, there is *knowledge*. As a historical religion, Christianity is based upon a knowledge of the activities of Jesus as a person in history. But one can believe all this and still not be a Christian:

> Faith also includes *assent* or *agreement* as to the significance of the facts. We agree that the historical record shows us to be sinners, both as individuals and as members of the human race. This disqualifies us from God's kingdom. We believe that Jesus who lived on earth was both God and man and that his death and resurrection have accomplished salvation for the entire world . . . but it still does not complete faith. One can agree to the truth of the Christian interpretation of facts and not be saved. James commented, "Even the devils believe—and shudder! They know the significance of what God has done, but they have refused to apply it to themselves."[2]

The most important aspect of faith is *trust*. Trust implies a reliance on and commitment to God, the giver of the gift. Faith is a relationship word more than a word describing what is true or false. To have faith is to be committed as a whole person to someone else.

Luther put it this way:

> There are two kinds of believing: first a believing about God which means that I believe that what is said of God is true. This faith is rather a form of knowledge than faith.... [Those] possessing it can say, repeating what others have said: "I believe that Christ was born, died, rose again for me." But what real faith is, and how powerful a thing it is, of this they know nothing....
>
> There is secondly a believing in God which means that I put my trust, . . . give myself up to thinking I can have dealings, . . . and believe without any doubt that [God] will be and do to me according to the things said of [God]. Such faith which throws itself upon God, whether in life or in death, alone makes a Christian.[3]

A popular illustration puts it another way. A crowd is gathered to watch a tightrope walker walk across Niagara Falls. The tightrope walker moves among the people and finally asks a woman, "Do you believe I can walk across?" She says she does, to which he responds, "Then let me carry you." Justifying faith in God is the kind that lets God carry us.

One further explanation may be helpful. Often we can better know what something means by looking at its opposite. Defining light as the opposite of darkness can be useful. Popularly, the opposite of faith would be disbelief or doubt. While linguistically that may be accurate, Søren Kierkegaard demonstrated that from a theological point of view it is misleading. Faith, he said, is a passion, and its opposite is *offense*. More than reason is involved. That element of emotional commitment or impact upon the whole person is illustrated by contrasting faith with offense.[4] To be offended is to be antagonistic in an emotional and intellectual way. David Read has suggested that because of Jesus' frequent questioning of the disciples about why they were afraid, Jesus saw fear rather than doubt as the opposite of faith.[5] The point is the same.

Now if salvation is genuinely a gift, it is important that faith not be regarded as a prerequisite to receiving salvation. Charles Anderson explains, "One is accepted through faith, not because of, or after faith. The difference is crucial for if I maintain that I am justified because of faith, the faith becomes a meritorious act or virtue by means of which I have a claim on God."[6] If we return to the gift analogy, faith is the reception of the gift that has been given. From a common sense point of view that is hardly a meritorious act.

There is one more difficulty in understanding faith. Christians believe that even faith itself is God's gift. Luther said in the meaning of the Third Article of the Apostles' Creed: "I believe that I cannot by my own understanding or effort believe in Jesus Christ my Lord, or come to him. But the Holy Spirit has called me."[7] But if God is responsible for faith, why do some believe and some not? Is there double predestination whereby God arbitrarily decides who will have a relationship with the divine and who will not?

One answer to this puzzle is that it appears from different points of view that both God and the person are acting. "In prospect we feel it is all up to us, but in retrospect we know that it is all of God…. Psychologically, prospectively, linguistically we enter the faith movement as the actor in the drama; theologically, retrospectively and spiritually, we know who its author is."[8] This argument is like the argument that it is futile to debate whether or not we have free will because we live our lives as if we do and as if our decisions make a difference.

A story may make the dilemma of human freedom and God's full activity in faith less confounding.

> Suppose there is an owner of a small business who happens to be very racist. He has a position open for an assistant and one day a Puerto Rican comes to him and asks for employment. Will he get the job? From a theological perspective, we can say the following: The businessman is held in bondage by his racism. He finds it impossible to relate to people in a non-racist manner. Of his own, he could not react lovingly and responsibly to the Puerto Rican by offering the job. But God, in his providence, is at work here. Seeking to enable all people to live in love, God is here challenging the racist *through* the challenge of the prospective employee. That is, the call of the man for the job is the call of God to be responsible. God is involved—but the decision must be made by the man. If he refuses to offer the job, he has freely made a decision to remain in bondage to his racism. If he says "O.K., the job is yours," then something new happens. A relationship is established between two people which is and becomes genuinely human, a relationship of love and responsibility. It is *through* this relationship that God now enables the persons involved to continue in love. By analyzing the matter in this way, both human freedom and divine power are related in a creative manner. The full depth of human sin is recognized, but the awful doctrine of double predestination is avoided.[9]

Good works

Quite often when we have developed a relationship with someone and found that person to be especially generous toward us, our response is to want to do something in return. A staff worker in campus ministry was leaving to go to Indonesia as a missionary. After he sold his home, a group of those whom he had helped showed up to clean the house as the staff worker moved out. They seemed delighted to do it. Tasks that might otherwise have been disliked were done joyfully because they were signs of gratefulness.

Luther said that the same kind of thing happens to Christians as a result of their faith:

Now after that a [person] is once justified and possesses Christ by faith and knows that he is [one's] righteousness and life, doubtless he [or she] will not be idle, but as a good tree will bring forth good fruits. For the believing [one] has the Holy Spirit, and where the Holy Spirit dwells, the spirit will not suffer [people] to be idle, but stirs [them] up to all exercises of piety and godliness, and of true religion, to the love of God, to the patient suffering of afflictions, to prayer, to thanksgiving, to the exercise of charity to all."[10]

The Augsburg Confession put it simply: "Our churches also teach among us that such faith should produce good fruits and good works and that we must do all such good works as God has commanded, but we should do them for God's sake and not place our trust in them as if thereby to merit favor before God."[11]

George Forell made the distinction between doing good work in order to receive a reward and doing it as a response to a gift that has been received:

If you truly believe God loves you and all other [people] unconditionally, a life of love and service will result. If you really believe that your sins are forgiven, you are enabled to forgive those who have offended and hurt you. This method is not the way we train animals; if you want to teach a dog a trick, you reward him after he has rolled over, stood on his hind legs or barked. If you give him a dog candy first, he will not do a thing. The Augsburg Confession claims that God treats us like [people], not like dogs, forgives us our sins and shows us [God's] love first, and expects us then to forgive and show love to others.[12]

As a believer, one has not simply a new status, but a new life; not simply a new attitude or new state of mind, but a new action; not simply a new situation, but a new person. God has acted so that the believer can "thank, praise, obey and serve" God.[13]

Grace-full relationships

What then is the shape of this life of gratitude that comes in response to God's gifts? First, having received grace, Christians tend to be grace-full in their relationships to others. Having received forgiveness for their shortcomings and not gotten what was rightfully theirs, Christians are able to be less demanding about what is due them.

Often we think of being grace-full in grand and cosmic terms, but Robert Herhold put a down-to-earth meaning to grace:

> Grace is someone breaking his or her back to help us and then replying with a smile, "No problem." Grace is someone saying "Have a good day," with a smile bursting through the cliché. Grace is being patient with a person we will never meet again and knowing we never will. Grace is being kind to a waitress who is wearing tight shoes. Grace is being nice to someone selling insulation over the telephone. Grace is the extra second we give to the driver ahead of us when the light turns green.[14]

Doing more than what is required

Second, the grateful believer seeks to do more than what is required. I recall when my stepfather had open-heart surgery at the same time the family was preparing for my sister's wedding. There was much to do, and ordinarily I would have been hassled by those extra demands, living an hour away as I did with a busy job of my own. But my mood at that time was such that nothing was too much to ask, as I was grateful that my stepfather was still alive.

There are Christians who play life according to the rules of the game. They obey the laws, observe the good customs, and do their fair share. Then there are others who play way beyond the rules. They do not ask what is their fair share. They see an opportunity to serve and give of themselves untiringly. When they are done, they do not quibble about the credit; they haven't time. They are already busy with some other good task.

The life inspired by gratitude frees one from the preoccupation of proving or justifying oneself to God by obeying divinely given laws. Ultimately more love will result. For love can never be commanded. Frederick Buechner wrote:

> By applying external pressure, I can make [people] do what I want [them] to do. This is [humanity's] power. But as for making [them] be what I want [them] to be, without at the same time destroying [their] freedom, only love can make this happen. And love can make it happen not coercively, but by creating a situation in which, of our own free will, we want to be what love wants us to be.[15]

That internal desire is what frees Christians to do more than is expected out of gratitude.

Freedom

Third, the life of gratitude is a life of freedom. John Vannorsdall put it well:

Freedom sometimes takes the shape of death.
To be free from the compulsions of love
   or the demands of justice
untouched by the cry of a child
   or the needs of its parents
untouched by the awe of gathering storm
   or stillness at dusk
unmoved by the terror of war
   or the prospect of peace
to be without the strings of remembrance
   or the bonds of hope
without a desire to work
   to lead or create
without expectations
   passions or goals
to be this totally free is, for us
   the shape of death.

Unable to remain aloof and live
   we naturally become involved
now serving those we love
   and subject to their death
rejoicing in our children
   and subject to their leaving
touched by compassion
   but threatened by its cost
compelled by the call of justice
   yet afraid of involvement
remembering before the fireplace
   made afraid by a knock at the door
now happy at the beauty of things
   but tormented by its passing
confident glance at the mirror
   but afraid of what we see
secure in growing pension
   but threatened by the future
confident we can decide
   and knowing that we won't
now freedom somehow disappeared
   and there's the tyranny of things.

Among those not free
   a voice cries:
"Freedom is born of being loved by one
   who is himself free
comes when you receive a love
   which is a gracious self-giving
comes from a love great enough
   to bear the cost of love
comes of a love
   which is not a tyrant's demand
comes of a self-giving
   which is free of subversion
is born not of a refusal
   to be involved in the world
comes neither of a yielding
   to persons and things
comes rather of response
   to the self-giving Christ
freedom is born in wonder
   at the suffering God."

Being loved we are set free
   to be involved.
Since our god is not ourselves
   we are free to be ourselves
our hope is not in our children
   we are free to love our children
our god is not our neighbor
   we are free to have a neighbor
our remembrance is not the source of life
   we are free to remember
since our goodness is not decisive
   we are free of the tyranny of goodness
our sin is not decisive
   free of the tyranny of sin
our status is not job-given
   free to do our work
our god is not tomorrow
   free for present joy
our fear is not of death
   free for present living.
Since our captivity is to the love of God
   we are really free . . .
   to be involved.[16]

Seeing differently

Fourth, gratitude to God helps believers see life from a different perspective. Michel Quoist, a French priest, said:

> If only we knew how to look at life as God sees it, we would realize that nothing is secular in the world, that everything contributes to the building of the Kingdom of God. To have faith is not only to raise one's eyes to God to contemplate [God]; it is also to look at the world with Christ's eyes.
>
> If we had allowed Christ to penetrate our whole being, if we had purified ourselves, the world would no longer be an obstacle. It would be a perpetual incentive to work for [God] in order that, in Christ, [God's] kingdom might come on earth as it is in heaven.[17]

Quoist's point is that if we personally know God as the giver of all good gifts and as the maker of all things, then we could perceive messages or gifts in creation if we looked at it differently. Quoist, for example, looked at green chalkboards and found in them reason to give God thanks for painting the forests and hillsides green, because green is restful to the eyes.

Our gratitude specifically for Christ's death on the cross suggests a number of possibilities. As offenders against the law, we were forgiven. Can we see those who have offended against the law as in need of the same mercy? As Christ conquered the violence of the battle between God and the powers of evil by suffering, can we begin to see the violence of our times as invitations to absorb violence in our suffering? If the cross was the means to reconcile us to God, are not occasions of strife invitations for us to become agents of reconciliation, even at personal cost? What we have received from God can change our whole perception about our circumstances and our relation to them.

A story illustrates this. "Once a man approached three bricklayers. He asked each the same question, `What are you doing?' The first said, `Making a buck.' The second answered, `Laying a brick.' And the third replied, `I'm building a cathedral.'"[18] How we regard what we're doing and how we are able to relate it to God will affect the satisfaction we receive from it as well as the resources and motivation we bring to it.

Decision making

The Christian also has a new perspective on decision making. The overriding motivation for Jesus' death on the cross was love. Our gratitude toward God leads us to want to relate to others with that same love. Luther put it this way:

> There must also be love. And through love we must do unto one another what God has done unto us through faith. For without love, faith is nothing....God does not want hearers and repeaters of words, but doers and followers, who exercise themselves in faith that works by love, for a faith without love is not enough, for it is not faith at all, but a counterfeit faith, just as a face seen in the mirror is not a real face, but merely a reflection of a face.[19]

Luther simply reflected the Bible by saying that love is the guiding principle for Christians. Jesus summarized it with the law to love the Lord our God and our neighbors as ourselves (Matthew 22:36–40). We read in the epistle of John that loving our neighbor is a prerequisite to claiming that we love God. Paul put love as the highest gift of the Spirit.

However, talking of loving and knowing how to love are two different things. My father had nephritis, a kidney disease that is terminal if untreated. The doctor told him that he had no more than three years to live. However, he could go on dialysis, which would prolong his life indefinitely. The cost was enormous. He could have a kidney transplant for three times as much. My father chose to have neither. He had a wife and a ten-year-old daughter. He felt it was his responsibility to work as hard as he could and supplement the savings he had so that both of them could be cared for after he died. To use up his savings on dialysis or a transplant would be selfish. I disagreed with him, arguing that his life could not be measured in dollars and cents and that what he could offer to his wife and daughter in the years he lived was far more important than anything he could leave behind.

Which one of us was right? More importantly, which choice is more loving? For the believer there is some help in making that decision and giving some shape to love.

First, the Bible has numerous commands that are expressions of love. In my father's case, "You shall not kill" is applicable, particularly when we add Luther's interpretation that we violate the command not only when we hurt our neighbor in any way, but also when we fail to "help him (or her) in all his (or her) physical needs."[20]

Second, we have the example of Christ. In my father's case, he would argue that Christ said, "No one has greater love than this, to lay down one's life for one's friends" (John 15:13). He did just that on behalf of his family. Giving up living was for him a way of loving wife and daughter.

Third, there is the general principle that the Christian is free. "For freedom Christ has set us free . . . do not submit again to a yoke of slavery" (Galatians 5:1). Luther expressed this as one-half of the ethical dialectic in his "Treatise on Christian Liberty": "The Christian is perfectly free, lord of all, subject to none."[21]

But the other side of the dialectic is just as strong: "The Christian is a perfectly dutiful servant of all, subject to all."[22] Here Luther reflected Paul's notion in 1 Corinthians and Romans that Christians are often called upon to give up their freedom in order not to offend less certain fellow believers. While certain behavior may not be immoral in itself, for the sake of others it should be avoided in some situations.

Fourth, as Christians we must be risk takers. Robert Jenson said, "To believe in this God is to believe that the calculable probabilities are not the whole story about what will happen."[23] Jesus' resurrection showed that God can act against the odds. Since Jesus was raised, anything can happen. If we believe God acts in history and is one agent who can and does shape events, then decisions must take into account the possibility of God's taking part.

Finally, linked with the notion of Christian freedom is the promise of forgiveness. My father chose to die. I thought he made a bad decision. Both of us thought carefully in order to determine God's will. While the responsibility to seek God's will is present in every circumstance, the assurance that forgiveness is promised to all who choose unwisely lifts some of the burden we feel in having to make these hard choices.

These aids to working out what love means make it possible to avoid two traps into which believers persistently fall. One is the trap of *legalism*, which endeavors to develop laws for every situation. It is always more comfortable to have a decision made in a clear-cut fashion by some external authority than it is to struggle with a complicated ethical question. Life has more gray areas than most people would like to admit. The more one knows about any situation, the grayer it seems to be.

The other pitfall is *antinomianism*. Some Christians, aware that they are free from the law, now believe they may do as they please. Luther's division of the Scripture into Law and Gospel and his insistence that one of the tasks of the Holy Spirit is to empower us to joyfully obey God's commands made it clear how opposed he was to this point of view. For him it was a rejection of the gift of the Word to want to make decisions without consulting the Word.[24]

So the Christian lives in tension between being grateful for the freedom that God gives and grateful for the guidance and direction of the law, the scriptures, and the call to servanthood. In that tension, love is forged.

At once sinner and justified

As hard as someone tries to live the life of gratitude and love, sin still seems to keep popping up. The satisfaction of having made some progress soon turns to spiritual pride. Paul bemoaned: "I do not do the good I want, but the evil I do not want is what I do.... Wretched man that I am! Who will rescue me from this body of death? Thanks be to God through Jesus Christ our Lord! So then, with my mind I am a slave to the law of God, but with my flesh I am a slave to the law of sin" (Romans 7:19, 24–25).

Some Christians believe that with the power of the Holy Spirit working in the believer, perfect life can be achieved. They take their justification from 1 John 3:9: "Those who have been born of God do not sin, because God's seed abides in them; they cannot sin, because they have been born of God."

Others believe that the improvement of the moral life is possible, as one moves progressively away from sinning. Paul wrote, "Not that I have already obtained this or have already reached the goal; but I press on to make it my own, because Christ Jesus has made me his own" (Philippians 3:12). The Christian life is a movement toward the ideal in Christ.

Luther accepted neither of these positions. For him Christians are at all times sinners and justified. The righteousness that justifies them is not their own, but Christ's. The more one works to love the neighbor or to draw closer to God, the more sensitive one becomes to areas of sin and parts of one's being kept from the lordship of Christ. So while some sin may disappear, other sin will emerge. So the believer is *simul justus et peccator* (at once sinner and justified) until Christ returns and the new heaven and new earth arrive.

By faith, then, Christians receive the gift of salvation from God. Their lives and their lips overflow with thanksgiving in the form of good works, grace-full relationships, going the second mile, a new perspective on things, and choices based on love. Herbert Tarr captured the sense of how the Christian responds to God's great gift in his novel *The Conversion of Chaplain Cohen:*

> David looked at his aunt and uncle—she, with hands chapped and hard from selling fruits and vegetables outdoors in all kinds of weather, the face ruddy and round and invariably smiling, the heavy body more accustomed to half a dozen sweaters at one time than a single coat, the hair the color of moonlight now, but the dark eyes still bright; he, with his slight wiry body strong and bent from lifting too many fruit and vegetable crates for too many years, the windburned skin, the swarthy face impassive except for the wry mouth—the childless couple who had taken the orphaned David into their home, rearing him since the age of seven, yet refusing to be called "Mama" and "Papa" for fear that he would forget his real parents.
>
> David grabbed their rough peddlers' hands in his smooth student ones. "How can I ever begin to repay you two for what you've done for me!" Uncle Asher spoke gently: "David, there's a saying: 'The love of parents goes to their children, but the love of these children goes to *their* children.' "
>
> "That's not so!" David protested, "I'll always be trying to—" Tante Dvorah interrupted. "David, what your Uncle Asher means is that a parent's love isn't to be paid back; it can only be passed on."[25]

That goes for God's love as well.

— 5 —

The Community
of the Gifted

*"But each of us was given grace according to the measure of
Christ's gift" (Ephesians 4:7).*

The year my mother received a new set of golf clubs for Christmas was
a watershed for her in many ways. She was basically a nonathletic person
who had given up all sports activities when her children came along.
Now that they had moved into homes of their own, she had time to do
something just for the fun of it.

Who would have been able to predict that the golf clubs would bring
a whole new group of friends? She joined a club and took lessons from a
pro. She also joined a women's group that played in foursomes once a
week. Soon couples from that group were staying afterward to have dinner together. The full integration of that group into her life became
apparent when she chose to spend New Year's Eve with them at the club.

Some gifts, by their very nature, encourage gathering with others
who have the same gifts. Computer clubs are springing up everywhere
in response to the home computers families receive as gifts. Musical
instruments received as gifts produce the same phenomenon.

So it is not surprising that a gift so much more central to a person's
life as salvation should also result in "a gathering of the gifted," a
community of those who have received the same gift from God, the
giver. This community is called the church.

But the comparison of the church with any voluntary association breaks down quickly. The gift that members of the church share has come to them from the church. For only as the gospel is preserved and spoken can God's gift come to anyone new. The God who gives the gift is God the Holy Spirit, who calls the church into being and continues to give it life. There is no choice as to whether gifted people join the church. They are the church.

I learned that lesson the hard way. When I arrived in college as a freshman, I had come from a high school where all the school leaders, athletes, and gung-ho types were involved in a Christian fellowship and where Christianity was for the attractive and successful students whom others admired. The fellowship I found at college was pallid by comparison. The women were social rejects (at least by my evaluation). The men were stuffy intellectuals wrapped up in the "pygmy world of personal piety," hiding in the fellowship because they were afraid to be corrupted by the fun of their classmates. What a motley bunch we made. I griped and complained that there was no way we could ever make an appealing witness to anyone who had anything on the ball.

Then I read *Life Together* by Dietrich Bonhoeffer. Bonhoeffer contended that Christian community is based not on my image or anyone else's image of what it ought to be. Such images he called "wish dreams." Rather, Christian community is based on Jesus Christ, and him alone. Those whom God places in any location are the Christian community. Christian community is, not an ideal, but a divine reality. My response to those who are Christians in any place ought to be to give thanks that they are there, being aware that Christian community is a privilege. I ought to be rejoicing that I did not need to profess the faith alone. God could speak to me through these people as well as any others. My whole attitude toward the group changed—and so did our fellowship.

If wanting the group to conform to my ideal was one error I made in regard to Christian community, expecting a certain kind of human interaction was another. Far too often I looked to the Christian community as a place to go where we gave "warm fuzzies," or positive strokes, to one another. I wanted a kind of human intimacy and closeness that felt good. Bonhoeffer insisted that Christian community must be a divine reality and not a human reality. We must be bound together by our faith and not by our warm experience, by our allegiance to Christ and not by our desire for intimacy. Only then, he said, can we experience the kind of love that accepts individuals as they are, as Christ accepts them, and that loves even the enemy in spite of how incompatible these people may be on the human level. "We are bound together by faith, not by human experience."[1]

According to the Augsburg Confession, there are two marks of the gathering of the gifted, the church: "It is also taught among us that one, holy Christian church will be and remain forever. This is the assembly of all believers among whom the gospel is preached in its purity and the holy sacraments are administered according to the gospel."[2] The church is the place where the gospel is preached and the sacraments are rightly administered.

Proclamation

The proclamation of the Word and the sacraments are known as "the means of grace" because they are the ways that God comes to us, the means by which Christ gives himself and by which the gifts God gives are bestowed. Right preaching of the gospel brings the gospel story into the present and causes it to be good news for us as it was when the story was first told. With all kinds of preaching and proclaiming going on today, how can one determine whether the gospel is preached "in its purity"?

Robert Jenson suggested two criteria for preaching in purity. "Authentic gospel . . . is talk of Jesus which is: (1) faithful to the remembered history, and (2) true response to the freedom of the risen Lord, acting in the lives of hearers as promise rather than as law."[3] Thus, to be true to the remembered history, proclamation is based upon the scriptures which the church has collected. To these scriptures the church has given its seal of approval, as being faithful to the history told over and over by the people of God. The service of worship is full of responses and hymns that have biblical texts as their source. The scriptures are read at worship. The sermon is an explanation of those lessons so that Jenson's second condition may be fulfilled in the lives of the hearers. One test of the authenticity of the gospel proclamation is its faithfulness to the tradition.

The second criterion is a bit more elusive to ascertain. Does the message come across with a promise of freedom in the risen Lord? Clearly some sermons do not. When the focus is on human sin and the message full of "oughts" and "shoulds," the message is received as bad news. Guilt, rebellion, and depression result. On the other hand, the remembered tradition can be preached in such a way that new possibilities, hope, and opportunity are what strike the hearer. Promises, said Jenson, are utterances that "pose a future in a very particular way: as gift."[4] Whenever the future is perceived as gift rather than threat because of the story of Jesus and Israel, authentic proclamation of the gospel has taken place. The notion that self-defeating behavior need not result in punishment, but can be confessed and forgiven, with the power to live differently, is an example of freedom rather than threat.

Proclamation does not occur only as a part of worship. Often the most effective proclamation is done by laypeople. Elton Trueblood reported that when he gathered twenty-five laypeople together and asked them what had influenced them to move from a nominal association with Christianity to a full commitment, without exception their response was "another person."[5] Gabriel Marcel said, "I am obliged to bear witness because I hold as it were, a particle of light, and to keep it to myself would be equivalent to extinguishing it."[6]

In some societies, religion and politics may not be considered polite topics of conversation. Nevertheless, for Christians to share themselves in any depth, they must share the source of their life and hope. Advertising saturation through television has made it routine to speak out about favorite products. "Sharing" experiences of getting rid of "ring around the collar" ought to make talking about overcoming alienation, guilt, or rebellion a refreshing change. The same criteria of authenticity that are applied to proclamation within the worship setting apply wherever the gospel is spoken. Is what we tell true to the remembered history, and does it promise an open future to the hearer?

Proclamation also has a corporate dimension. The church as a gathered community often needs to speak forth its message in relation to controversial issues in society. For example, the gospel has a clear message about racial equality, and Martin Luther King, Jr., was a man motivated by the gospel to inspire others to speak forth firmly on that issue. That proclamation is true to the tradition that says that in Christ "there is no longer Jew or Greek, there is no longer slave or free, there is no longer male and female; for all of you are one in Christ Jesus" (Galatians 3:28).

That proclamation holds the promise of a future free from bondage to prejudice and discrimination of the parties on both sides. The corporate proclamation reveals to the public that the God who delivered Israel delivers still. The issues of ecology, peace, and justice for women are the kinds of human concerns that benefit from a gospel perspective. To be silent is to betray the God who has given so much to all people.

Jesus commanded Christians to proclaim the gospel not just where they happened to find themselves but "to the ends of the earth" (Acts 1:8). Jesus said, "Go therefore and make disciples of all nations, baptizing them in the name of the Father and of the Son and of the Holy Spirit, and teaching them to obey everything that I have commanded you" (Matthew 28:19–20). One result for the church has been foreign missions. Individuals have been called by God and the church to live in foreign countries to tell the story of Jesus, proclaiming its message of freedom to all people. Schools, hospitals, and relief agencies have been established around the globe to make the proclamation of the gospel tangible as well as verbal. Most of the leadership in Africa today was educated in schools established by Christian missionaries.

When proclamation is done responsibly, the message of the gospel must be distinguished accurately from its Western cultural trappings. When it is not, the church is guilty of its own form of paternalism and colonialism. However, the positive reception of the gospel in every part of the world in the nineteenth century is evidence of the universality of its message and of the God to whom it bears witness.

George Macleod, abbot of the Iona community in Scotland, summed up the outward thrust of proclamation:

> I simply argue that the cross be raised again at the center of the marketplace as well as on the steeple of the church. I am recovering the claim that Jesus was not crucified in a cathedral between two candles, but on a cross between two thieves; on the town garbage heap; on a crossroads so cosmopolitan that they had to write the title in Hebrew and Latin and Greek (or shall we say in English, in Bantu and in Afrikaans) at the place where cynics talk smut, and thieves curse, and soldiers gamble, because that is where he died and that is what he died about. And that is where church people should be and what church people should be about.[7]

The sacraments

The second mark of the church is the right distribution of the sacraments, Baptism and Holy Communion. In Augustine's words, the sacraments are visible words, the gospel proclaimed in a drama. They are the gospel acted out. The sacraments are holy acts, instituted by Christ, which use earthly visible signs to bestow the grace of God. It is this definition that determines that there are two, rather than seven, sacraments as the Roman Catholic Church contends. All of the other five rites (confirmation, holy orders or ordination, marriage, reconciliation or absolution, and the anointing of the sick, formerly known as extreme unction) do not meet all the requirements of this definition of a sacrament. Marriage, for example, was instituted by God and practiced long before Christ came and has no visible sign prescribed as essential to it. Thus these five rites do not have the same prominent and indispensable place in the life of the believer as Baptism and Holy Communion.

Baptism

The sacrament of Baptism is the initiation rite into the family of God. It was commanded by Christ in Matthew 28:19–20. The visible sign is water, and the promise made by God is that "one who believes and is baptized will be saved" (Mark 16:16).

Differences among Christians about Baptism largely focus on who is the primary actor in the sacrament. For Luther, the actor is God who cleanses the baptized, gives the baptized the Holy Spirit, and frees the baptized from the power of death and the devil. All this is accomplished by God through water and the Word. Baptism is the quintessential demonstration of the grace of God, the giver, bestowing on those who neither deserve nor merit its life-giving gifts. Thus the youngest infants can be baptized, these gifts can come to them as well.

Churches that practice "believer's baptism" (the descendants of the Anabaptists in the Reformation) focus on the faith of the believer. Baptism is the ceremony that follows a profession of faith in Jesus as Lord. Only those who can understand what faith in God is and make that profession of faith are eligible for baptism—the one "who believes and is baptized will be saved," they read in Mark 16:16.

Similarly, the amount of water used in baptism has differed among Christians. The baptism of John, and presumably of all the early Christians, was by immersion. When Paul wrote in Romans 6:4, "Therefore we have been buried with him by baptism into death, so that, just as Christ was raised from the dead by the glory of the Father, so we too might walk in newness of life," he called on the symbolism of going under the water into death and then rising out of it to newness of life. Many Christians believe that the amount of water is not important. Water used with God's Word is all that is required. Thus, living outside a warm climate, away from rivers and lakes that were accessible year round, people found other containers for water. Soon immersion was no longer practiced. But the effect of Baptism was the same.

How much water is used may not be an issue, but the use of water is crucial. For the symbolism of water in God's dealings with the Israelites as well as the Christians is all meant to be recalled as the baptism occurs. A baptismal prayer refers to these symbols:

> Holy God, mighty Lord, gracious Father: We give you thanks, for in the beginning your Spirit moved over the waters and you created heaven and earth. By the gift of water you nourish and sustain us and all living things.
>
> By the flood you condemned the wicked and saved those whom you had chosen, Noah and his family. You led Israel by a pillar of cloud and fire through the sea, out of slavery into the freedom of the promised land. In the waters of the Jordan your Son was baptized by John and anointed with the Spirit. By the baptism of his own death and resurrection your beloved Son has set us free from the bondage to sin and death, and has opened the way to the joy and freedom of everlasting life. He made water a sign of the kingdom and of cleansing and rebirth. In obedience to his command, we make disciples of all nations, baptizing them in the name of the Father, and of the Son, and of the Holy Spirit.[8]

As water was the means for bringing order to chaos, so Baptism brings order to the chaos of lives today. As water nourishes and sustains all living things, so believers are nourished and sustained by remembrance of their baptism. Israel was delivered through the water of the Red Sea, so the baptized are delivered through water. As Jesus was anointed with the Spirit at his baptism, so the baptized receive the Spirit today. The splash of water can evoke this in those familiar with the tradition.

Luther did not regard Baptism as a once-and-for-all act. In the Small Catechism he wrote: "What does Baptism mean for daily living? It means that our sinful self, with all its evil deeds and desires, should be drowned through daily repentance; and that day after day a new self should arise to live with God in righteousness and purity forever."[9]

Luther retook his baptismal vows daily. The effects of one's baptism continue, but they do so in part by recollection. Thus, in a baptismal liturgy, the entire congregation is called upon to recite the Apostles' Creed with the person being baptized and renew their baptismal covenant on a regular basis. To live as a baptized person is to live with a confidence about one's identity and a certainty of God's claim on one's life. To remember one's baptism is to hear in one's mind, "You are baptized," at every point of temptation, doubt, and despair. The objectivity of the act apart from one's faith, the piety or lack thereof on the part of the pastor, or one's age make it the kind of event that is an anchor on which one can rely when all else seems unreal.

Yet infants are not able to renew their baptismal covenant on a regular basis. How can baptism be meaningful for them? Luther's argument for infant baptism was that

> God has sanctified many who have been thus baptized and given them the Holy Spirit.... Since God has confirmed baptism through the gift of the Holy Spirit, as we have perceived in some of the [leaders] such as St. Bernard, Gerson, John Hus and others who were baptized in infancy...our adversaries must acknowledge that infant baptism is pleasing to God. For [God] can never be in [internal] conflict, support lies and wickedness, or give [God's] grace and spirit for such ends.[10]

Luther further argued that it is God and the water and the Word that are active in Baptism. The faith of the believer is not the issue. Even if faith is the issue, infants may be believers. It cannot be satisfactorily demonstrated either that they are or are not. Moreover, infants are as much in need of cleansing from sin as any others, for sin is the condition into which all humanity has been born as a result of the fall. The gift of God's initiative and acceptance into a relationship comes most vividly when an infant is baptized.

In summary, the community into which one is baptized is crucial. An infant cannot verbalize what it means to be a member of a family but learns it inductively as that reality is lived out. In the same way, what it means to be a member of God's family is learned inductively as the community nurtures and models life in relation to God.

The Lord's Supper

The Lord's Supper, which is also called the Holy Eucharist, the Sacrament of the Altar, and Holy Communion, is the family meal of the people of God. Gathered at the communion table, Christians are fed *by* Christ, who is the host at the meal, and *on* Christ, who gives both forgiveness of sins and himself to each person there. As such, participation in the Lord's Supper is as central to the life of faith as breakfast, lunch, and supper are to our biological lives. Indeed, in the early church Holy Communion was celebrated every Sunday.

The command of Christ instituting the Lord's Supper was recorded in three of the Gospels and in Paul's first letter to the Corinthians:

> The Lord Jesus on the night when he was betrayed took a loaf of bread, and when he had given thanks, he broke it and said, "This is my body that is for you. Do this in remembrance of me." In the same way he took the cup also, after supper, saying, "This cup is the new covenant in my blood. Do this, as often as you drink it, in remembrance of me."[11]

Bread and wine are the visible signs, and the promise is forgiveness of sins, life, and salvation.

The debate among Christians has always been on the meaning of the words "This is my body . . . this is my blood." The Roman Catholic Church at the Council of Trent in 1551 contended that when the words of institution were spoken, a miracle took place in which the bread and wine were changed into the body and blood. To explain this phenomenon, the Roman Catholics appealed to Aristotelian metaphysics to say that the "substance" of the elements changed, but the "accidents" remain the same. All things, like an apple, have accidents: color—red, green, or yellow; taste—sweet or sour; and so forth. These may change, and it will still be an apple, but the substance is the "appleness," which must be unchanged or the apple becomes something else. In Communion the substance of the bread and wine change, but the accidents remain the same; it still appears to be bread and wine. Traditionally this view has been called "transubstantiation." Currently, Roman Catholic theology has been considering the emphasis of the action of the community as the heart of the Eucharistic celebration.

Luther, on the other hand, said that when we eat and drink it is perfectly obvious that it is bread and wine we consume. Nevertheless, Christ has also promised to be present *in* them. So the communicant must receive Christ "in, with, and under" the elements. He is present "to forgive, to save, to unite, to give life, to comfort, and to strengthen for the work to which he calls his people in the world."[12] Luther avoided the question of *how* Christ is present. Christ's promise is believed and the mechanism marveled at for its mystery.

A third view of the Lord's Supper has Christ present—not in the meal itself—but in the memory of the believers. Communion is celebrated to recall the Last Supper and to bring to mind the sacrificial death of Christ on the cross. It is a memorial meal. Baptists, for instance, and some other Protestants are likely to hold this view.

The sacrament of the Lord's Supper is as rich in symbols as is Baptism. The meal was instituted as a Passover supper Jesus had for the disciples the night before he died. The Passover supper celebrated the deliverance of the Israelites from Egypt. The Israelites were permitted to leave Egypt after the Lord had slain all the firstborn children in Egyptian households but "passed over" the homes of the Israelites, which were identified with the blood of a sacrificial lamb on their doorposts. Jesus is the Passover lamb for Christians. When John the Baptist introduced Jesus to the first of the disciples, he said, "Here is the Lamb of God who takes away the sin of the world!" (John 1:29). Those same words are part of the service of Communion, sung just before believers receive the bread and wine.

The bread and cup symbol has been a sign of unity in the church. If the bread is Jesus' body, then all who partake of it are one body in Christ. In congregations where disagreements and factions seem inevitable, this affirmation of unity has often been the source of reconciliation. One Communion I will always remember found a Laotian refugee at the altar rail beside a feminist theologian, who was next to a judge who had been unseated because he declared a plaintiff in a sexual assault case had provoked the rape. All three ate from one loaf.

The sacrament also has a future dimension. It is a foretaste of the heavenly banquet promised to believers:

> There was a great multitude that no one could count, from every nation, from all tribes and peoples and languages, standing before the throne and before the Lamb, robed in white, with palm branches in their hands. They cried out in a loud voice, saying, "Salvation belongs to our God who is seated on the throne, and to the Lamb!" (Revelation 7:9–10).

The heavenly banquet is a celebration of the final victory over evil, when there will be no more divisions or tears or death, and God will not come hidden in bread and wine, but be openly present for all to see. The future dimension of the sacrament inspires hope.

Again, in the Lord's Supper the gift-nature of salvation is made apparent. There is no way humans could develop a ritual that would allow them to receive Christ regularly, but Jesus instituted Holy Communion and gave it to his followers as a gift. Once again, that gift is the giving of himself.

The power of that meal can never be fully explained, nor should it ever be underestimated. Gregory Dix said:

> For century after century, spreading slowly to every continent and country and every race on earth, this action has been done, in every conceivable human circumstance, for every conceivable human need from infancy and before it to extreme old age and after it, from the pinnacles of earthly greatness to the refuge of fugitives in the caves and dens of the earth. [People] have found nothing better to do for kings at their crownings and for criminals going to the scaffold; for armies in triumph or for a bride and bridegroom at a little country church; for the proclamation of a dogma or for a good crop of wheat; for the wisdom of the Parliament of a mighty nation or for a sick woman afraid to die; for a schoolboy sitting in examination or for Columbus setting out to discover America; for the famine of whole provinces or for the soul of a dead lover, in thankfulness because my father did not die of pneumonia . . . for the repentance of Margaret; for the settlement of a strike . . . on the beach at Dunkirk; while the hiss of scythes in the thick June grass came faintly through the windows of the church . . . one could fill many pages with the reasons why [people] have done this, and not tell a hundredth part of them. And best of all, week by week, month by month, on hundreds of successive Sundays, faithfully, unfailingly, across the parishes of Christendom, the pastors have done this just to make the *plebs sancta Dei*—the holy common people of God.[13]

We need the sacraments to make faith real beyond all thoughts and works and prayers and songs. We need them as we need touches and embraces in order to be in love. God knows this, and that is why they are God's gift to us.

A sacramental vision

One result of receiving God's gifts is a new way of seeing. For those for whom the sacraments have a central place in life, that way of seeing has a special twist. Activities in life become "sacramental" in that they can be viewed as occasions when God's grace becomes manifest in tangible ways. Tom Woodward, an Episcopalian priest offered a quiz to stimulate that kind of thinking:

Which of the following are sacraments or sacramental?
- an embrace
- ironing someone else's shirt
- cutting down a tree
- a gift of a handful of jellybeans from a five-year-old
- coffee hour after church
- a trip through an art museum
- a peace march
- a gathering in support of a particular war
- a wedding
- bandaging a child's hurt finger
- psychiatric counseling[14]

If your answers to any of the above is "no," what would make that a sacrament (or sacramental)? If your answer to any of the above is "yes," what would make that other than a sacrament (or sacramental)? The sacramental vision is an elaboration of Jesus' view of the world expressed in parables. The church is like a vineyard. God is like a waiting father. When we look at life through God's eyes, events can point to God and God's ways of relating to the world.

One, holy, catholic, apostolic

The church is defined in the Augsburg Confession as the community of believers where the Word is rightly preached and the sacraments rightly administered. The Nicene Creed describes it: "We believe in one holy, catholic and apostolic church."

That the church is *one* goes against all the empirical evidence. There are more than four hundred denominations in the United States alone. But the unity of the church is not organizational. Rather, the church is one because, as Paul said, "There is one body and one Spirit, just as you were called to the one hope of your calling, one Lord, one faith, one baptism, one God and Father of all, who is above all and through all and in all" (Ephesians 4:4-6). All Christian churches confess Jesus Christ as Lord, and the denominations then become the many parts of the body of which he is the head.

However, the confession that the church is one is also an expression of hope. There is no indication that there will be denominations in heaven. The ecumenical movement has worked to bring the unity which the churches confess into tangible manifestation. All Christians have incentives to work toward that goal. First among those is the witness such visible unity would make to the world. If Christ was right in saying, "By this everyone will know that you are my disciples, if you have love for one another" (John 13:35), then the unity of the church is a testimony to that love.

The church again can be regarded as *holy* only from a dialectical perspective. All Christians are made holy by the sacrifice of Christ's blood. They put on the righteousness of Christ, which is theirs as a gift, having no righteousness of their own. In this sense the church is holy.

On the other hand, the church is a human institution, and like all human institutions, sinful. It does not always do God's will. It fails to behave in loving ways both to its members and to those outside. Often it seeks to preserve itself rather than give itself for the life of the world. So just as the Christian is at once justified and sinner, so the church is at once holy and corrupt. The Apostles' Creed calls it the communion of saints, but a confession calling it the communion of sinners would be equally accurate.

Catholic is a word that has caused great confusion to Protestants. As a generic term it means universal. The church must be open to everyone. Paul said, "As many of you as were baptized into Christ have clothed yourselves with Christ. There is no longer Jew or Greek, there is no longer slave or free, there is no longer male and female; for all of you are one in Christ Jesus" (Galatians 3:27–28). There can be no American church or women's church or black church or socialists' church. All people of every description are welcome into Christ's body, and Christians in every part of the world are part of it. In first-century Jerusalem the battle began. Could male gentiles enter the Christian church without being circumcised? Could people enter without first becoming Jews? The council at Jerusalem overwhelmingly decided that there was not a different gospel for the gentiles. Again, this description does not always coincide with perceived reality. Too often churches have become fellowships of the like–minded. The whole idea of neighborhood churches militates against this universality. If individual congregations do not mirror catholicity, at least worldwide Christianity does.

The church is not coextensive with the members of all the congregations in the world, however. Christians call this the visible church, but the true church (in another one of these dialectics, that is the only accurate way of speaking about so many things with which

God has to do) is invisible. Not all who are members of the institutional church are members of Christ's body. Jesus warned, "Not everyone who says to me, 'Lord, Lord,' will enter the kingdom of heaven" (Matthew 7:21). There may be some who are not a part of the institutional church but who do enter into a relationship with God. Classically, the thief on the cross to whom Jesus promised, "Today you will be with me in Paradise" (Luke 23:43), is an example. Some Protestant churches have made an effort to screen out those who do not appear to be part of the true church in order to make their fellowship pure. Yet others have chosen to leave the judgment of salvation to God. Recalling the parable of the wheat and the weeds (Matthew 13:24–30), they obey Jesus' admonition to wait until the harvest to do the sorting, lest in gathering the weeds good wheat is also uprooted. So the church is universal, and except to God its true composition is invisible.

Finally, the Creed describes the church as *apostolic*. When earlier in this chapter I made an effort to establish the criteria for determining proclamation that is pure, I listed faithfulness to the remembered tradition as one guideline. To say that the church is apostolic is to say that it preaches the gospel of the apostles, those who had firsthand, or at most secondhand, accounts of the life and teaching of Jesus. John said:

> We declare to you what was from the beginning, what we have heard, what we have seen with our eyes, what we have looked at and touched with our hands, concerning the word of life—this life was revealed, and we have seen it and testify to it, and declare to you the eternal life that was with the Father and was revealed to us (1 John 1:1–2).

Since New Testament times, some people have preached another gospel. Any new teaching must be substantiated by the account of those who were closest to Jesus. To maintain an identity, any organization must have a statement of belief. Apostolicity is the criterion for including one thing rather than another in that statement in the church.

The gifted gathering

The gift of salvation and a renewed relationship to God are not the only gifts bestowed upon the believer. The sacraments are gifts. But the Holy Spirit also gives other gifts to be used for the building of the church. Two lists of these gifts appear, one Romans: "We have gifts that differ according to the grace given to us: prophecy, in proportion to faith; ministry, in ministering; the teacher, in teaching; the exhorter, in exhortation; the giver, in generosity; the leader, in diligence; the compassionate, in cheerfulness" (Romans 12:6–8).

The second list is in 1 Corinthians:

> Now there are varieties of gifts, but the same Spirit; and there are varieties of services, but the same Lord; and there are varieties of activities, but it is the same God who activates all of them in everyone. To each is given the manifestation of the Spirit for the common good. To one is given through the Spirit the utterance of wisdom, and to another the utterance of knowledge according to the same Spirit, to another faith by the same Spirit, to another gifts of healing by the one Spirit, to another the working of miracles, to another prophecy, to another the discernment of spirits, to another various kinds of tongues, to another the interpretation of tongues. All these are activated by one and the same Spirit, who allots to each one individually just as the Spirit chooses (1 Corinthians:12:4–11).

Because the lists are different, we can assume that neither is exhaustive, but each is meant to indicate a full range of abilities useful to the church with which the Holy Spirit equips believers. We can also assume, then, that because the Holy Spirit gives different gifts to different people, the church cannot function properly unless all people are exercising the gifts God has given them. Therefore, part of being a member of the church is discovering one's special gifts from God and using these for the common good.

Followers of Luther generally have been so concerned about justification by faith and the centrality of Christ that one hears little about this work of the Holy Spirit. Those were the kinds of concerns that "charismatic" (from the Greek word *charisma*—meaning "gift") or Pentecostal churches might emphasize. In the Reformation period those who focused on these gifts placed the authority of the Word in subordination to the private revelations of the Spirit. But today one of the signs of life in the church is the renewed attention to lay ministry and the work of the Spirit. It is always dangerous to despise the gifts of God. F. D. Maurice said, "I cannot but think that the reformation in our day, which I expect to be more deep and searching than that of the 16th century, will turn upon the Spirit's presence and life, as that did upon the justification of the Son."[15]

Stewardship

I still remember Christmas as a five-year-old. I received my first two-wheel bicycle, the largest present I could remember ever receiving. I had hardly gotten over my elation and surprise when my father said, "Now you'll have to show us you're big enough to take care of this, or it will be taken from you." My father was a bit quick on the trigger, but I did develop a sense that the larger the gift received, the greater the responsibility that goes with it.

Christians refer to this responsibility for what they have been given by God as *stewardship*. Peter wrote, "Like good stewards of the manifold grace of God, serve one another with whatever gift each of you has received" (1 Peter 4:10). The Greek word for steward could be translated "trustee." It referred to the one who administered a household, especially the pantry, kitchen, and dining hall, but often the clothing and other needs of the family as well. Jesus used the word when he explained to Peter his responsibility for all he had been given. "Who then is the faithful and prudent manager whom his master will put in charge of his slaves, to give them their allowance of food at the proper time?" (Luke 12:42).

The Bible refers to all people and all creation as the whole inhabited earth for which God has made them responsible. If Luther's meaning of the Fourth Petition of the Lord's Prayer is taken into account, the provider of the bread has a rather wide job description. "What is meant by 'daily bread'? Daily bread includes everything needed for this life, such as food and clothing, home and property, work and income, a devoted family, an orderly community, good government, favorable weather, peace and health, a good name, and true friends and neighbors."[16]

Christians exercise this stewardship in a variety of ways. Giving proportionately of one's income, following the biblical injunction to tithe is one way. The church uses this money to support service projects, world relief agencies and educational institutions, and to provide materials that help guarantee that God's varied gifts are distributed to those in need.

Increasingly, Western Christians understand that giving is not sufficient to fulfill their responsibilities as stewards. What is at issue is *lifestyle*. To deplete or pollute the earth's resources so that generations yet unborn will not have them available is bad stewardship. To eat more than necessary while people starve in the world is bad stewardship.[17]

To purchase nonessential products that are available cheaply only because labor is exploited in another part of the world is bad stewardship. To support a government budget that increases the percentage spent on defense and decreases the percentage spent on aid to the poor is bad stewardship. To use more fertilizer on golf courses in our country than we ship to India for agricultural use is bad stewardship.

Augustine said: "Find out how much God has given you, and from it take what you need. The remainder is needed by others. The superfluities of the rich are the necessities of the poor. Those who retain what is superfluous possess the goods of others."[18]

Because the world's population has grown so large and projections indicate accelerating increases, the whole issue of how to share the gift of the earth, the gift of creation is central to a Christian's response today. Sharing that gift is crucial to establishing even a shaky peace. Wars over resources are quite possible in the future. With nuclear capability extended to more and more nations, the possibility of a major planetary disaster initiated by struggles over resources becomes more likely. How to preserve the earth under these circumstances and to share its resources equitably may be the major questions for Christians today. Christianity is the only institution with members in all countries of the world. That provides marvelous opportunities. The Lord's admonition in terms of stewardship becomes a challenge: "To whom much is given, much will be required."

For Christians, then, whether the family has meat for dinner, sets the thermostat lower in winter, or buys new clothes are not just economic questions. They are questions of what it means to be good stewards of God's varied gifts. The church, then, is the community of the gifted where the gifts of Word and sacraments and the gifts of the Spirit are received and shared. It is a community gathered by God, the giver, where God is worshiped and received, and where we are empowered to act on God's behalf in giving to one another and the world.

— 6 —

The Care of the Gift

"If you knew the gift of God, and who it is that is saying to you 'Give me a drink,' you would have asked him, and he would have given you living water" (John 4:10).

One year my daughter received a St. Bernard for Christmas. She was delighted, but she soon discovered that this was not a gift that could be put on the shelf and admired. The dog had to be walked several times a day, regardless of the weather. Samson, as she called him, needed food and water daily, without fail. His long hair got dirty and tangled easily, so she brushed him. Most unpleasant of all was cleaning up the "messes" in the backyard. Yet the more she took care of Samson, the more attached she and he became.

Salvation, the gift from God, is more like Samson than it is like a book or a new sweater. While salvation is given freely, the relationship with God requires care and attention if it is to be maintained or, better yet, to grow. Christians have talked about this care as the cultivation of spirituality. Involved in this growth is discovering those things that give us contact with God so that our experience of God is alive and vital and nurturing.

Spirituality has two sides. It involves, first, hearing what God may want to communicate to us, and then sharing what we want to communicate to God. Just as relationships with others are sustained by meeting together, by listening, and by sharing, our relationship with God grows in the same way.

Waiting on God

The Bible teaches that while some encounters with God come as surprises—like Moses and the burning bush or Saul on the Damascus road—others come only after a period of patient waiting. "My soul waits for the Lord more than those who watch for the morning," says the psalmist (Psalm 130:6). Israel waited forty years to enter the Promised Land. Christians have waited for nearly two thousand years for Christ to return.

Since waiting is not something our modern culture affirms, it is a part of spirituality we may need to learn. Waiting on God is different from waiting in rush hour. There we feel like a passive victim. To wait on God is an active choice, not imposed from the outside. Henri Nouwen says that the people waiting in Scripture

> know that what they are waiting for is growing from the ground on which they are standing. That's the secret. The secret of waiting is the faith that the seed has been planted, that something has begun. Active waiting means to be present fully to the moment, in the conviction that something is happening where you are and you want to be present to it. A waiting person is someone who is present to the moment who believes that this moment is *the* moment.[1]

I had an experience in London that gave me insight into how waiting actively and expectantly can make a difference. I often would go to the theater and sometimes wait for three hours for "returns," tickets people would bring back or not pick up for that night's performance. I disliked the process sufficiently that I would endure it only for the very best of shows. Then one night while waiting for tickets for *Les Miserables* I discovered that a person ahead of me in line was from my hometown in the United States. I was eager for news. We talked, discovered mutual friends, and the time passed quickly. After that I looked forward to waiting in line because I went anticipating that someone unexpected but interesting might be there. I had learned to wait actively.

To wait for God requires patience. In a microwave society where everything is measured in minutes, getting into the mindset of Abraham, who waited a lifetime for the promised heir, or of Joseph, who spent many years in prison before being tapped to run the nation for Pharaoh, or of Simeon, who waited his lifetime to see the Messiah, is difficult. But there is no instant spirituality any more than there are instant human relationships. As we wait with and for God, the Spirit works in and with us to bring growth, change, and faith.

Growth in spirituality takes time, which seems to many the most valuable possession they have. Habakkuk was impatient in his day. "O Lord, how long shall I cry for help, and you will not listen?" (1:2). He longed for God to remove the injustice among the nations. But he learned to wait, "for there is still a vision for the appointed time; it speaks of the end, and does not lie. If it seems to tarry, wait for it; it will surely come, it will not delay" (2:3). God will not disappoint those who wait.

Solitude

A second prerequisite for spiritual growth is solitude. Too often the business of life makes so much background noise that we would not be able to hear God if God spoke directly to us. Jesus' withdrawal to a mountain to pray and Elijah's hearing God in "the still small voice" suggest that a place alone where it is quiet may be where our relationship with God is nurtured. I know parents who spend time alone with each of their children each week because they know things will be shared under those circumstances that never would be shared with the whole family together. Couples take second and third honeymoons to get back in touch with one another. In the same way, time alone with God is needed to nurture that relationship.

Many find that getting away from other people, the telephone, the television, and the radio does not in itself produce quiet and solitude. For once the external distractions have been put aside, the inner chaos becomes all consuming. Our anxieties, fears, doubts, bad memories, unresolved conflicts, and impulsive desires suddenly seem to rush upon us. We have often chosen to be busy in order to have good excuses for not dealing with these feelings. When we are alone, these issues begin filling our mind and our attention. Henri Nouwen once again puts this dilemma into perspective:

> One of the early Christian writers describes the first stage of solitary prayer as the experience of a man who, after years of living with open doors, suddenly decides to shut them. The visitors who used to come and enter his home start pounding on his doors, wondering why they are not allowed to enter. Only when they realize they are not welcome do they gradually stop coming. This is the experience of

anyone who decides to enter into solitude after a life without much spiritual discipline. At first, the many distractions keep presenting themselves. Later, as they receive less and less attention, they slowly withdraw.[2]

We find solitude the same way we find anything else important in our lives: we schedule it. For some, a place is important—a room with a phone that can be unplugged and a lock on the door, or an empty church, or a spot in the woods. The time spent in solitude can grow as desire for it increases. But the goal is to be in a spot physically and emotionally where we can hear the voice of God.

Thirsting for God

The most fundamental step we can take toward opening ourselves to a relationship with God is to discover our longing for God, our yearning for God's fullness in us and in the world. The psalmist writes: "As a deer longs for flowing streams, so my soul longs for you, O God. My soul thirsts for God, for the living God" (Psalm 42:1–2). Luther says in his explanation to the Third Article of the Creed that even this longing is the work of the Holy Spirit.

The desire for God is present in everyone but sometimes needs to be aroused. The contention of the believer is that although people search for fulfillment through pleasure, power, love, or relationships, the ultimate longings of the heart are for God and will not be satisfied in any other way. Rudyard Kipling was speaking for everyone when stirring restlessly in a serious sickness, he answered the nurse's query. "Do you want anything?" with the murmur, "I want God."[3]

This thirst for God is often born out of some crises. When extreme danger comes—as in wartime, or serious disease, or the loss of a family member in death—often a person turns to God in anger, asking, "Why me?" or for seeking help, asking for resources beyond those that can be mustered internally to deal with the situation. Our own drought turns us to the source of living water.

In my own case, the divorce of my parents when I was a teenager awakened in me a thirst for God. At that time I prayed in a desperate way I had never prayed before and received the peace for which I asked. Some time after praying I read in the psalms, "If my father and mother forsake me, the Lord will take me up" (Psalm 27:10), discovering the promise that had just come true for me. From that time on my thirst for God was whetted. My longing to know God better would grow.

Listening for God

Relationships grow as a result of communication. We wait for God, we find a place and attitude of solitude, we cultivate a thirst for the Almighty in order to be able to receive God's communication to us. How then can we hear what God has to say?

The primary means of hearing God's word to us is by reading the Bible. Luther declares that the work of the Holy Spirit is to take the text of the Scriptures and bring it alive for us. The Spirit is able to transform the words of the Scripture from history or poetry written hundreds of years ago into a love letter as fresh as if it arrived today. In that letter God communicates with us, God addresses us today. For this reason the Scriptures are often called the Living Word. Daniel Erlander has written:

> Truth is the living, creative, powerful address of a loving God. Truth is the Living Word which breaks into ourselves, into our history, shattering old ways and creating *new life, new values,* and *new commitment.* Living Word is the "address" that created change. Living Word is like the plea of an old-fashioned young man on his knees asking a young woman to marry him. She realizes that her affirmative response to this "address" will change the rest of her life.... through Christ, God woos and pleads with us, "I love you. I forgive you. I want you. Trust me. Obey me. Enter the joy of my kingdom." When we hear this call, we hear the *Living* Word.[4]

In hearing that Living Word we are hearing God communicate with us through the Scriptures.

The approach to reading the Bible that is most likely to achieve this end differs with the individual. Luther favored reading large sections of Scripture at a time until something in the text addresses you. Don't be worried about what you can't understand. You can understand more than you will ever put into practice. In another reading at a later date, other parts may make sense. That would be his advice.

Others advocate taking a short segment of Scripture and reflecting upon it until God's voice can be heard through it. Take for example,

John 1:14, 16: "And the Word became flesh and lived among us, and we have seen his glory, the glory as of a father's only son, full of grace and truth.... From his fullness we have all received, grace upon grace."

From that verse one of these phrases can be selected for meditation:

- The Word became flesh
- Lived among us
- We have seen his glory
- Full of grace and truth
- From his fullness
- We have all received

Focus upon the phrases, allowing the Spirit to bring to mind the many layers of meaning and association in each phrase. The riches come from mining one vein very deeply rather than a much larger range on the surface.

There is a middle ground as well. Many books are available that suggest a short reading from the Old Testament, a short reading from the Epistles, and a short reading from the Gospels for every day. The readings may have a common theme, or they may each be leading continuously through a book of the Bible. With this approach, the reading of three passages may make it seem more likely that God can address individual situations through what is read. Most communities that have daily worship services follow this pattern. Finally, by reading four chapters a day, the whole Bible can be read in one year.

Meditation

Having read the Scripture, we meditate on it to hear God speaking to us. Dietrich Bonhoeffer wrote:

> In our meditation we ponder the chosen text on the strength of the promise that it has something utterly personal to say to us for this day and for our Christian life, that it is not only God's Word for the Church, but also God's Word for us individually. We expose ourselves to the specific word until it addresses us personally. And when we do this, we are doing no more than the simplest, untutored Christian does everyday; we read God's Word as God's Word for us.[5]

The great temptation that comes from reading the Scriptures and expecting God to speak from them is that we measure whether God is speaking by how we feel or what new insight occurs. Like any relationship, our relationship with God has occasions when we learn something about God that is genuinely moving. But most days, as in any relationship, the communication deals with truths that are important but not new or surprising in any way. On those days it is the regularity of our involvement, our reassurances that we are loved or are on the right track, the very familiarity that confirms in us that we are close. The effectiveness of God's communication with us may be just as clear if it is something we have heard before as if it is some new insight. That we tell our children "I love you" as we tuck them in to bed every night does not make it ineffective communication every night after the first time. That message builds self-esteem and security just because it has been spoken over and over again. God's love, God's forgiveness, God's power, and God's will become part of our being and something we know about God for sure only as we hear it over and over again.

One great aid to meditation is memorization. Scripture we have memorized we can recite over and over again to ourselves at all sorts of times and places. The Spirit can bring it to mind when we need to hear its message. In the same way that circumstances set off certain "tapes" from our parents—pieces of homespun wisdom or perhaps criticism—so verses we have memorized can be the means God uses to address present circumstances.

In any case, meditation is work. Meditation involves using all our intellectual and intuitive ability to discover God's message to us in the present. Those who learn biblical languages, read commentaries, and check cross-references, with the goal of understanding a biblical passage in its context, are helping the process by which God addresses them through those words today. Until I traveled from Boston to Baltimore with a geologist who pointed out the rock in every cut made for the road and what it meant about the prehistory of that locality, I never noticed the differences. Now I never miss them. Studying a text can open us to see messages from God we might otherwise miss.

Prayer: Our communication with God

Having prepared ourselves and having heard God's word addressed to us, our side of the conversation that builds the relationship with God is called prayer. Although we may turn to God because we are overwhelmed by the beauty of creation, or because we or someone we love is in desperate need of help, or because we are grateful for an undeserved blessing, from Luther's point of view the reason to pray is simpler: God commands us to pray. The proper response to a command is obedience. So we pray. In his commentary of Matthew 6:5–6 Luther wrote:

> I have often taken up and discussed the component parts and the characteristics which every real prayer has to possess, and therefore I shall only summarize them briefly here. They are as follows: first, the urging of God's commandment, who has strictly required us to pray; second, [God's] promise, in which [God] declares that [God] will hear us; third, an examination of our own need and misery, which burden lies so heavily on our shoulders that we have to carry it to God immediately and pour it out before [God], in accordance with [the] order and commandment; fourth, true faith, based on this word and promise of God, praying with the certainty that [God] will hear and help us—and all these things in the name of Christ, through whom our prayer is acceptable to the Father and for whose sake [God] gives us every grace and every good.[6]

Luther focused on the command to pray, which we should obey, and the promise that our prayers should be answered, which we should believe. This is characteristic of how Luther understood the gospel.

For some the process of prayer does not come easily. Questions about how a mortal sinner can address the all-powerful God, of whether prayers don't really bounce back off the ceiling, or of whether prayer is not some psychological trick, so engage some people that they cannot begin uttering the first words. Here some of the discipline of solitude that clears one's own mind of the inner chaos may prove helpful.

But the question of what to say in prayer still may be a puzzle. We learned to speak by imitation. How many times did we listen to someone else say "Daddy" before we could say it ourselves? So using the prayers of others may be the best way to start to pray.

The Psalms are prayers of people in almost every circumstance of life. Psalm 136 is a prayer of thankfulness. Psalm 22 is the prayer of one who feels forsaken by God. Psalm 70 is a prayer for help. Psalm 63 asks for God's presence. Psalm 51 is a prayer for forgiveness. Reading the psalms often brings forth the very words we want to speak to God.[7]

Other prayers can be found in Scripture. Paul's letters often begin with thanksgivings, long prayers of thanks for the particular qualities or deeds of the people he addresses. When the disciples wanted to pray, Jesus taught them the model prayer that has become known as the Lord's Prayer (Matthew 6:9-13). We can both pray that prayer, which is a great summary of all we might want to say to God or use it as a pattern for creating prayers of our own.

Outside the Bible, the worship books of most churches are filled with prayers for every circumstance. The prayers of the faithful through the ages have been preserved, and by imitating them we can learn what may seem new or strange as we begin.

Prayers generally fall into four basic categories, which can be remembered as the ACTS: adoration, confession, thanksgiving, and supplication. *Adoration* is praising God for who God is. Often this is a good way to begin prayer because it focuses on God instead of ourselves. We can express God's power, faithfulness, love, and promises of deliverance in adoration.

Most services of worship have prayers of *confession*, which provide a model for our individual prayer. In confession we make amends with God. By and large, individual prayers of confession are specific, expressing the precise deeds, attitudes, or failures that trouble our conscience. *Thanksgiving* prayers involve gratitude. One of the tasks of meditation is pondering how the circumstances in our lives can be used for good and become occasions for thanksgiving.

Finally, there is *supplication*. Even those who generally pay little attention to God pray for help in times of need. If our relationship with God is like that of a child to a parent, then it is altogether appropriate that it include many requests. These prayers of supplication also are ways of demonstrating our reliance upon God.

As we have learned in solitude to wait and listen to God, we respond to God with prayers that a we have learned from Jesus, from others who have been faithful, and finally from our hearts. As surely as with any friend, the more the communication flows the closer we become. As we reveal our innermost thoughts and desires, we allow God into our lives more. In the end, we discover the joy of being called God's friend.

— 7 —

The Gifts
Yet to Come

"The free gift of God is eternal life . . ." (Romans 6:23).

Some gifts are first experienced in anticipation. They are promised for a special occasion in the future. My first car was that way. My parents did not permit me to have a car while I was in college, but they promised from the time I got my driver's license that they would give me one for graduation. Much of my daydreaming focused on all the things I would be able to do once I had that gift.

Some of the gifts that God gives can only come in the future, for they have to do with a history not yet experienced. Theology talks about them under the category of *eschatology*—the doctrine of the last things. In the Apostles' Creed, Christians express their belief that Jesus will come again to judge the living and the dead. The creed also speaks of "the resurrection of the body" and "the life everlasting," God's future gifts. Christ will bring with him the gift of a new kingdom of peace and righteousness for which people through the centuries have longed. He also will bring the gift of continued personal existence, the resurrection of the body "to all who believe in him."

Before examining these gifts in detail, the importance of knowing as much as possible about the future needs to be addressed. I found out the hard way. In art class I was given a bar of Ivory soap from which I was to carve a sculpture. With my limited ability, I thought the only thing I would be able to make would be a small model of the

Washington Monument, but I began to chip away, hoping that something would emerge. The result was a pile of shavings. The fact that the incident was a parable was not lost on me. My hopes for the future had a lot to say about my actions in the present.

Sociologists and theologians have stronger statements about the importance of expectations for the future. Some are saying that a major ideological shift occurred in the 1960s. In that decade people stopped looking to the past for direction and began looking to the future. The transition was fostered in part by the emerging ecological concern that without present planning there might not be air and water on the planet in the near future. Academicians began to research areas to help instigate change in the future. Businesses began to pay high wages for a breed of thinkers called "futurologists," whose job was to dream about the future. Science-fiction writers became the authors of bestsellers. At the same time theologians began to use the Christian understanding of the future as the center of their thought. The task of the Christian was to bring that hoped-for future into the present. This cultural change, then, inaugurated an era when the future had more impact on the present than ever before in history.

It is curious that people have to have some sense of the future or they die. The concentration camp experience demonstrated this in a powerful way. Viktor Frankl, a Jewish psychiatrist incarcerated at Auschwitz, wrote about a composer who was in the camp with him. "The prisoner who had lost faith in the future—his future—was doomed. With this loss of belief in the future . . . he let himself decline and become subject to mental and physical decay."[1] This prisoner had a dream that on March 30 the war and the suffering would be over for him. On the night of March 29, he became ill with a high temperature. The next day he became delirious and lost consciousness. On March 31 he died. Frankl, who served as a medical doctor in the camp, asserts that when liberation did not come, the prisoner lost hope and courage. His bodily resistance went down, and he died of typhus. Faith in the future is necessary for life.

The return of Christ

German theologian Hans Schwarz wrote:

> It has become evident that, while we may be able to survive some of the thunderclouds that loom threatening in the horizon of history,

lasting hope cannot come from within us. While we can always achieve temporary victories, ultimately death will stare us in the face. When we give account of the hope that is in us, we can only do so because it has been placed in us from beyond our time-bound world. Any tenable hope for the future thus cannot rest on us, but must be affirmed by the God who created the world, does sustain it, and will eventually redeem it.[2]

The return of Jesus Christ is the guarantee that all God's promises for a kingdom where peace and justice are fully manifest, where the lamb and the lion can lie down together, and where sorrow and weeping and crying are no more, will come true. All three Synoptic Gospels prophesy Christ's return (Matthew 24, Mark 13, Luke 21). From the point of view of the atonement, Christ's return will secure the victory over all the evil forces in the great cosmic battle between God and Satan. From the historical point of view, the return is a guarantee that history will have an end as it had a beginning. The Christian understanding of history is not cyclical nor spiral-like. It is linear. C. S. Lewis once said that when the author comes out on the stage the play is over. Christ's second coming will be different from the first in that Christ will not be hidden, as he was in the babe in the manger. Rather, he will come victoriously in such a manner that all will recognize his divinity. At that time all creation, not just human life, will be new. John spoke of it this way:

> Then I saw a new heaven and a new earth; for the first heaven and the first earth had passed away, and the sea was no more. And I saw the holy city, the new Jerusalem, coming down out of heaven from God, prepared as a bride adorned for her husband. And I heard a loud voice from the throne saying, "See, the home of God is among mortals. He will dwell with them as their God; they will be his peoples, and God himself will be with them; he will wipe every tear from their eyes. Death will be no more; mourning and crying and pain will be no more, for the first things have passed away" (Revelation 21:1–4).

When this second coming will occur has been a matter of great speculation throughout history. The followers of Jesus expected it to happen before they died. Today people speculate that all the prophesied preconditions have been met. The Bible is clear that Jesus will come "like a thief in the night" (1 Thessalonians 5:2), "but about that day and hour no one knows" (Matthew 24:36). In regard to the time, Christians are admonished to "watch" and "pray," always ready for Christ to return.

The greatest result of the promise of Christ's return is that it provides a strong source of hope. No matter what catastrophe happens in our history, the end of history will be good. Christ ultimately will triumph over any evil humanity can concoct. For the Christian this means that despair over the state of the world should never be the last word, because God is in control and will manifest that control for good. Christians may not know all the future holds, but they know who holds the future. Thus, they have reason to hope.

The resurrection of the dead

Woody Allen is quoted as saying, "I don't mind dying. I just don't want to be there when it happens."[3] How to cope with mortality is a universal human dilemma. Peter Berger put it seriously: "Every human society is, in the last resort, [people] bonded together in the face of death. The power of religion depends . . . upon the credibility of the banner it puts in hands of [people] as they stand before death, or, more accurately, as they walk inevitably toward it."[4]

The Christian answer to death is the resurrection of the body. God who created human life in the first place will recreate it into something new after death. The entire person dies. There is no immortal soul as the Greeks propose, for that would mean people live on after death. Life after death, like life before death, is a gift of God. Only God has the power to make it happen.

David Redding made it seem absurd that God wouldn't make it happen:

> The end of the Creed is a logical development of its beginning. Maker of heaven and earth? Why? For us. For "life everlasting." God did not survey the building site here in space to begin with, saying: "What a marvelous place for my cemetery." Naturally dead [people] treat God as nothing better than a graveyard superintendent. The apostles wrote this live, not introducing God as a patient archaeologist waiting for the dust to settle on [God's] succession of civilizations so he can excavate and stuff his specimens. "[God] is not the God of the dead but the God of the living." [God] did not do earth to record it or tape it or get a good picture to remember us by. [God] is doing it live for keeps.[5]

What is the nature of the resurrected body? In 1 Corinthians 15, Paul gave us all we know about it. It is to be like Christ's resurrected body since he was the "first fruits of those who have died" (v. 20). The relationship to the earthly body is compared with the seed and what it produces (v. 36). It will be imperishable (v. 42). It will participate in glory (v. 43). It will have power where it was weak before (v. 43) and will be spiritual (v. 44). From this description it is apparent that, like Christ's resurrected body, our bodies will retain enough likeness for us to be recognized after the resurrection yet will have substantial differences. The resurrected body will be completely new.

Again, the belief in the resurrection of the body is not belief in any incubation process or scheme of metamorphosis. Rather, it is belief that death has been defeated, robbed of its power, and that the relationship one has with God will never be severed. Again, that brings hope for the future. For Paul it was central enough to the Christian faith that he could say if Christ wasn't raised, and the dead aren't raised, the gospel is null and void (1 Corinthians 15:14). Thus Christians sing Easter songs of triumph at funeral services and cannot only console those who remain, but also say with Paul, "For to me, living is Christ and dying is gain" (Philippians 1:21). In the face of death, Christians are able to celebrate the entrance of another saint into glory. Christians can risk their lives, as Dietrich Bonhoeffer and Martin Luther King, Jr., had done, for the sake of the gospel, for death is not the end. Those with painful diseases will not carry those pains with them forever. All these promises are from God. The new life to come is another of God's gifts.

The judgment

"He shall come to judge the quick and the dead," Christians confess in the Apostles' Creed. In Hebrews we read, "It is appointed for mortals to die once, and after that the judgment" (Hebrews 9:27). Jesus himself said, "The hour is coming when all who are in their graves will hear his voice and will come out—those who have done good, to the resurrection of life, and those who have done evil, to the resurrection of condemnation" (John 5:28–29). One of the most quoted parables of Jesus is the parable of the last judgment, when all the nations will be called before him and he will divide "the sheep from the goats" on the basis of the acts of mercy they have done or failed to do (Matthew 25).

The Day of Judgment is well documented, and Jesus will be the judge. From a practical viewpoint, that frees us from ever having to make the judgment about who is saved and who is not. We ought not judge, because to do so is idolatry, placing ourselves in the position of God.

Besides, the evidence to be used on that day seems to be different from what we might use. Works, that which we have done, seem to be the criteria suggested in one passage after another. Again, we might be inclined to give someone a quiz on doctrine to determine admission. Jesus, on the other hand, is judging from the perspective of "faith, by itself, if it has no works, is dead" (James 2:17). All faith that is genuine will bear fruit. Faith that saves is faith that has been integrated into our own being.

But what about hell? How can a loving God permit there to be a hell and that some will be left in a state of torment? Hell is a necessary condition for humans with free will. G. K. Chesterton made the case well:

> To the Buddhist or the Eastern fatalist, existence is a science or plan which must end up in a certain way. But to a Christian, existence is a story which may end up in any way. In a thrilling novel (that purely Christian product) the hero is not eaten by cannibals; but it is essential to the existence of the thrill that he [or she] might be eaten by cannibals. The hero must (so to speak) be an eatable hero. So Christian morals have always said to [humanity] not that [it] would lose its soul, but that [it] must take care that [it] didn't. In Christian morals, in short, it is wicked to call a [person] "damned"; but it is strictly religious and philosophic to call him damnable....
>
> Life (according to the faith) is very like a serial story in a magazine. The point of that story (life) is exciting because it has in it so strong an element of will, of what theology calls free will. You cannot finish a sum how you like. But you can finish a story how you like.... And Christianity has excelled in the narrative romance exactly because it has insisted on the theological free will.[6]

Put another way, God does not damn people to hell. People choose their destinies for themselves, and God respects their choices. Hell, however, is reaching that point where the decision cannot be changed and discovering that the choice is wrong. One of the functions of Jesus' return will be to make clear to all that he is Lord and that those who made that confession were speaking the truth. Helmut Thielicke said:

> As long as I don't know that from which I have been cut off, the separation really causes me no anguish.... But to have to look at the spring of life without being able to drink from it—that hurts. That is

to suffer the torment and exile from which there is no return....[7] When murderous King Claudius, in *Hamlet*, tries in vain to pray, he cannot break the evil spell of his own burning conscience. So he cries out, 'Pray can I not.' In this line Shakespeare has described hell exactly, and, in general, he shows an uncommon understanding of this dimension of torment."[8]

However, that is not the final word. Someone has said that while our reason and the Scriptures convince us there must be a hell, we can, nonetheless, pray to God that it be empty. God then saves some of the best gifts for last—God's coming again, the resurrection of the body, and the new heaven and the new earth. Our anticipation of receiving them is what the church calls hope.

— 8 —

The Gift That
Explains the Others

*"All scripture is inspired by God and is useful for teaching, for
reproof, for correction, and for training in righteousness"
(2 Timothy 3:16).*

Sometimes the goodness of others can be such a surprise that suspicion
develops about its authenticity. An elderly woman stopped in one day
at our campus center in Madison, Wisconsin, saying Jesus had told her
to come. If I would go to the local mall, she said, there would be a box
of shoes that she had bought, and Jesus wanted me to distribute them
to the students who needed them. Then she left.

Although the woman was obviously not Greek, immediately the
old saying, "Beware of Greeks bearing gifts" came to mind. But I did as
she said, brought the shoes, and quickly distributed them to the students.

The woman returned—once with a check to help buy food for our
cost suppers, then with mugs we could use for coffee. Just before
Christmas she bought a sofa for me. With every gift she warned that it
must never be refused. Suppose the sofa didn't go with anything I had?
Suppose this woman was getting these things illegally? Could this
woman be trusted?

Gradually I got to know the woman, a retired member of the
Women's Army Corps. who lived at the YWCA on her pension and
Social Security. Her life was devoted to listening to Jesus and giving

to people. All the merchants knew her, and she paid her bills on time. As unusual as her generosity was, it was genuine, authentic, strictly above board. There was no reason not to accept the gifts and give thanks to her—or, as she preferred, to God.

For some people the Christian faith seems too good to be true. That God would give all the things to humanity that it needs is a bit suspicious. Isn't it more likely, they would say, that people have created this scheme to satisfy their own needs? Is not Christianity just one more system of belief created by a culture to give divine sanction to the way it lives, a hoax now perpetrated by many others? Besides, reliance upon gifts from God undercuts human effort. Also, doesn't the disagreement among those who claim to be Christians and the apparent inequality of the gifts they have received indicate that these beliefs are not true?

Every set of proposed truths must have some authority, some basis for testing its validity. How can we know that the gospel story is true? Knowing the "shoe lady" over a period of time convinced me of her legitimacy. As our relationship grew, my trust in her and belief in what she said also grew. If the gospel is essentially about a restored relationship to God through Jesus, then the ultimate test for its validity will come from being part of that relationship and seeing if it lives up to what others say about it. There is no way of knowing for sure whether the gospel is an authentic gift without receiving it, trying it on, seeing how it fits. With some gifts we get thirty-day home trials. Perhaps that kind of option would be useful for the gift of the gospel.

What I am suggesting is that the gospel is self-authenticating. Because it has to do with a relationship, there is no provable data that will demonstrate its rightness. Someone may tell me about all the wonderful qualities of a friend, and I may have no reason to dispute them. Until I get to know the friend myself, however, I will never know if they are right. By its very nature the truth of the gift of the gospel is self-authenticating.

Revelation

Having said that, it is still possible to move the discussion back one step further. How do we know that there is a gift in the first place, as well as what the gift is? For Christians, the answer must be, "God told us," or at least, "God told some others whose accounts we believe." The source of knowledge about God and divine activity is *revelation*. That revelation comes in two forms: in Jesus and in the Bible. The Bible is the account of how God was revealed to the Israelites and through Jesus.

Revelation is a source of knowledge about God, just as science is a source of knowledge about the material world. Each is appropriate for its subject matter. Problems occur only when the approach of science is applied to things about God and vice versa. It is not that the Bible is unscientific, but that using science to get at the meaning of the Bible misses its main point. Both forms of knowledge begin with hypotheses. Science believes that the world is rational, orderly, and mechanical. Sometimes something is uncovered—like the Heisenberg principle of uncertainty—but the hypothesis is not abandoned. It still accounts for things "for the most part." The Bible claims to be revealed and can be read with that hypothesis in spite of small things—like historical contradictions—that may cause one to question that hypothesis.

The Bible

Part of deciding on the reliability of the gospel, therefore, has to do with coming to a conclusion about the Bible. According to the Formula of Concord, "We believe, teach and confess that the prophetic and apostolic writings of the Old and New Testaments are the only rule and norm according to which all doctrines and teachers alike must be appraised and judged."[1] The Reformation leaders were expressing an opinion about the Bible that had been present in the church through the centuries and taken for granted. Whenever councils had made decisions about heresy, the Bible was the norm to which the leaders turned to settle the question.

Why is the Bible so regarded? First, it testifies to Christ, who is ultimate authority. Luther liked to refer to the Bible as the manger in which Christ was laid. Alan Richardson also made this point:

> The authority of scripture consists solely in the fact that the Bible is the authoritative historical witness to Christ. It is the testimony of those who actually saw and witnessed to the saving acts of God in history.... This is the significance of both the Old Testament and of the New Testament. Both testaments witness to Christ: the Old Testament contains the testimony of the prophets to the Christ who

should come; the New Testament contains the witness of the apostles to the fact that Jesus of Nazareth is he. Outside the Bible there is no historical testimony to Christ; everything that can be known about the Jesus of history is to be found in it.

This is why the canon of the New Testament closes about the end of the first century A.D.; there is no more historical witness to be had, for those who had been in touch with the original eyewitnesses were now almost all passed from the scene. It is not a question of "progressive revelation" of ideas about God, but the testimony of eyewitnesses to the unique and saving act of God in history, the Christ event, which is the theme of the Bible as a whole.[2]

Scripture also makes some claims about its authority. "No prophecy of scripture is a matter of one's own interpretation, because no prophecy ever came by human will, but men and women moved by the Holy Spirit spoke from God" (2 Peter 1:20–21). "All scripture is inspired by God" (2 Timothy 3:16). "The word of the Lord came to me" is a phrase that recurs frequently in the Old Testament. "Thus says the Lord" is another. Jesus himself said, "The scripture cannot be annulled" (John 10:35). He spoke of himself as the fulfillment of scriptures (Matthew 26:54–56). Paul said, "Anyone who claims to be a prophet, or to have spiritual powers, must acknowledge that what I am writing to you is a command of the Lord" (1 Corinthians 14:37). The writers of the Bible perceived themselves as writing what God revealed.

Even revealed, the Bible remains a human book. It is actually a library of many books and literary genres written over a period of two thousand years. The style and concerns of each writer were not overridden. Each approached the witness to the acts of God in history a little differently. Some books are poetry, others chronicles, others visions. As diverse as the books of the Bible are, its unity is a marvel. Yet when two or three writers reported on the same event they gave different details, just as witnesses in court offer different details when they recall an event.

In the Bible we find the same paradox present in Christ. He is at once truly human and truly divine. So the Scriptures are both human documents and God's revelation. As the holy God was cradled as a human in the manger, the Word of God is cradled in the Bible.

Even these statements are statements of faith more easily made by a believer than an inquirer. For the Bible's authority, like the authority of the gospel, is self-authenticating. People discover that reading it gives light when the way seems dark. What was written centuries ago seems written just for them.

The most objective verification for the Bible is its historical accuracy. The life of Jesus and the development of a Jewish sect that followed Christ was well documented by secular historians. Archaeology continues to uncover papyri, artifacts, evidence of cities that both confirm the biblical record and aid significantly in its interpretation. W. F. Albright, professor emeritus at Johns Hopkins University, said, "There can be no doubt that archaeology has confirmed the substantial historicity of the Old Testament tradition."[3] It is amazing that such a statement can be made about writings that existed orally for long periods of time before they were recorded. The Bible, which is about God's activity in history, holds up well under historical scrutiny.

However, to read the Bible as a historical document is to miss the point. What is important about the Bible and its message is the *meaning* of certain events in history. The Bible was written to communicate God's role and activity in history, making that history crucial for life today.

The Bible, then, is another gift from God. We need not search for God or God's will any longer. Though we do not live in the time of Jesus in Galilee, the promise of God is that Jesus can be encountered still as we read God's book.

The confessions

For Christians the ultimate authority is Jesus Christ, the Lord. The Bible is the authority that makes him and his will known. Historically, though, even those who have confessed Jesus as Lord and looked to the Scriptures as authoritative have disagreed. By what they lift from the Bible as being most important, different groups of Christians distinguish themselves. These groups have written summaries of beliefs for use in public celebrations and in debates over true understandings of the gospel.

The creeds are three of these confessions. The Apostles' Creed is of uncertain origin but has roots in the old Roman creed of the third century. It may have had liturgical use before then. It summarizes the Christian faith. The Nicene Creed was written to combat the teachings of Arius and was adopted at the Council of Nicea in A.D. 325. It was modified slightly at the Council of Constantinople in A.D. 381. It makes the two natures of Christ more explicit. The Athanasian Creed is also of uncertain origin and deals more comprehensibly with the Trinity. Up to the Reformation, all found acceptance in all of Christendom.

In 1530, after Luther's protest against some of the teachings of the church, the princes and representatives of the free cities in the empire were invited by Emperor Charles V to Augsburg, Germany, to discuss their religious differences. The princes and representatives tried to demonstrate peacefully that the faith they preached was the faith of the Bible. The faith the church had always taught formulated the Augsburg Confession. Through the presentation of this confession they hoped to restore unity to the church.

Their effort failed at that time, but Roman Catholics today, following the reforms in that church at the Council of Trent and Vatican II, are able to say that the Augsburg Confession declares the faith they, too, preach and teach.

The confessions today function in the church as pointers, treasures, and anchors. They are pointers in that they point beyond themselves to the scriptures about Christ. They are treasures in that they represent the living tradition of the church. They show how believers in times past have summarized the gospel in light of their historical circumstances. They are like what Paul "delivered" in 1 Corinthians 15:4: "For I handed on to you as of first importance what I in turn had received." Like family treasures, they help continue telling the story of God's people. They are anchors in that they keep the church from getting too far adrift as it tries to give new expressions to the gospel. "By centering our thoughts on Jesus Christ, by calling us back again and again to this center, the confessions provide a footing against the currents, winds and tides that swirl around and within every believer."

To be a Christian one is not required to have faith in the Bible or in the confessions. No doctrine of Scripture was ever debated when Jesus called people to follow him. The gospel is a gift to be received without prerequisites. For those who have received this gift, God has provided others that they are likely to find useful—the Bible and the confessions of the church. They are maps for the journey and must not be confused with the journey itself. It is as one embarks upon that journey that the map is helpful. Paul Tournier wrote:

> The great gift, the only one which can be unchanging in value, is the assurance of life beyond the grave, of peace beyond remorse. It is the assurance of reconciliation with ourselves, with our neighbors and with God, beyond all the conflicts which have accompanied and tarnished the joys of our existence.

The great gift, the unique and living one, is not a thing, but a person. It is Jesus Christ himself.... This gift of all gifts is the self-commitment of God who carried it through to the bitter end so that we may entrust ourselves to it.

The almost unbelievable news of the revelation is that it really is a gift. It is free, without reservation and without recall. Whatever our virtues may be, whatever may be the times of our repentance, they all would be unequal to the payment of such a treasure. Thus it is that God offers it freely. [God] is the one who paid its price, in the death of [God's] Son. The erasure of all our failings and all our remorse, of all our regrets and rebellion, what a gift it is! The redemption of all our joys about to be swallowed up in death, and their fulfillment in eternal joy itself—what a gift indeed.[5]

Questions for Reflection and Discussion

The following questions may help you reflect on your own life, your beliefs, your doubts, your experiences. They will also help you understand the teachings in each chapter and apply them to your life. If you are studying this book as part of a group, you can use the questions to guide your discussion. You may also want to ask, "What did you find most interesting, helpful, or puzzling in this chapter?"

Chapter 1. The Giver

1. At this point in your life, what are the main questions you have about God?
2. Brainstorm and make a chart by asking, "How do you know God exists?" For each answer see what each piece of evidence says about God. For example: "I know God exists because of the feelings I have when I am in the mountains at sunset." The God known in this way is a creator God. "I know God exists because there is order in the universe" (argument from design). The God described this way is a proposition at the end of an argument. "I know God exists because God answered my specific prayer." The God known this way is personal and powerful.
3. How is the God revealed by acts in history different from the God known by philosophers? Which do you think is a better source of knowledge? Why?
4. How is revelation as a source of knowledge different from science as a method of gaining knowledge?
5. What do we learn about God from Jesus? What do we know about God from other sources?
6. How does the resurrection of Jesus have implications for the lifestyle and future of believers?
7. How do you understand the work of the Holy Spirit?

Chapter 2. The Receiver

1. How do you understand God's relationship to the created universe?
2. How are people different from the rest of creation? How would you define what it means to be a person?
3. How did Jesus show what it means to be truly human?
4. List all the synonyms for sin you can think of. In a parallel column determine the consequences of each synonym. To what extent can these synonyms be generalized as forms of death or disbelief?
5. How would you answer these questions: What is really wrong with human beings, individually and collectively? What does that have to do with the Christian concept of sin?

Chapter 3. The Gift

1. Which explanation of Christ's death makes the most sense to you? Why? What do the others contribute to our understanding of Jesus' death and resurrection?
2. In what circumstances has the assertion "Jesus died for me" made sense to you? From what have you been saved? Why? How?
3. If you could ask Jesus any questions, what would they be?

Chapter 4. Response to the Gift

1. What is one thing in which you "have faith"? How did you come to that faith, and what difference does it make? (Examples: education, parents, science.)
2. How do you know whether you have faith? What is it? How do you "get" it?
3. What are the rivals to Christian faith in your life and in the world?
4. How do you understand the relationship between faith and good works?
5. What are the characteristics of a life of gratitude? To what extent are you living such a life?
6. According to the author, there are two major pitfalls in the Christian life: legalism and antinomianism. Which is the greater danger for you?
7. What is the significance of saying that the Christian is both sinner and justified?

Chapter 5. The Community of the Gifted

1. What has been your relationship to the church? How do you feel about the Christian community in which you now find yourself?
2. According to Robert Jenson, what are the criteria for the right preaching of the gospel?
3. What is the Christian obligation to proclaim the gospel in a diverse pluralistic society?
4. What significance does your baptism play in your life?
5. How do you understand the presence of Jesus in Holy Communion?
6. In what ways is the Christian church one, holy, catholic, and apostolic?
7. What gifts do you have that can be used within the body of Christ?
8. How does the Christian concept of stewardship inform the current concern for ecology and earthkeeping?

Chapter 6. The Care of the Gift

1. Why does the gift of salvation require care and attention?
2. What does it mean to wait for God?
3. According to the author, what are the prerequisites for spiritual growth? To what extent are they now present in your life?
4. What method of reading and meditating on the Bible seems most valuable or possible for you?
5. Are there ways of listening for God in addition to reading the Bible?
6. What role does prayer play in your life now? What aids to prayer have you found useful?

Chapter 7. The Gifts Yet to Come

1. What plans or dreams for the future do you have that are affecting the way you live now?
2. "Faith in the future is necessary for life." How would you interpret that for yourself?
3. What changes in attitude or behavior result from a belief that Christ will return?
4. What is your attitude toward your own death?
5. What are the ramifications of believing in resurrection of the body rather than immortality of the soul?
6. What are your current beliefs about judgment, hell, and heaven?

Chapter 8. The Gift That Explains the Others

1. What role has the Bible played in your life?
2. What does it mean to say that the Bible is self-authenticating?
3. In what sense does the Bible reveal God?
4. What are the confessions of the church? How might they help you in your spiritual journey?
5. What are the major questions you still have about the Christian faith? (It's all right to have questions. That's how we grow.)

~ Notes ~

Note: All bracketed words found within quotations were not in the original texts but were added to include people of both genders.

Introduction

1. Paul Tournier, *The Meaning of Gifts* (Atlanta: John Knox, 1966), 52.
2. Henri J. Nouwen, *With Open Hands* (Notre Dame, Ind.: Ave Maria, 1972), 64.
3. Dietrich Bonhoeffer, *Cost of Discipleship* (New York: Macmillan, 1959), 45–60.

Chapter 1

1. J. D. Salinger, *Franny and Zooey* (New York: Bantam Books, 1955), 170–71.
2. Martin Luther, *The Small Catechism* (Minneapolis: Augsburg, 1968), 12.
3. Marbury Anderson and Frank Klos, *I Believe in Jesus Christ* (Philadelphia: The Lutheran Church Press, 1965), 123.
4. Ethelbert Stauffer, *Jesus and His Story* (New York: Alfred A. Knopf, 1960), 17.
5. Sir Edward Clarke, letter to E. L. Macarsey, as quoted in John Stott, *Basic Christianity* (Downers Grove, Ill.: InterVarsity Press, 1958), 47.
6. Luther, *The Small Catechism*, 10.
7. Stephen Neill, *Christian Faith Today* (Baltimore: Penguin Books, 1956), 79–80.
8. G. Ernest Wright and Reginald Fuller, *The Book of the Acts of God* (Garden City, N.Y.: Doubleday, Inc., 1960), 7, 15.
9. Luther, *The Small Catechism*, 13.
10. Dorothy Sayers, *Creed or Chaos?* (New York: Harcourt Brace, 1949), 135–36.

11. C. S. Lewis, *Mere Christianity* (New York: Macmillan, 1943), 135–36.
12. Theodore Tappert, ed. and trans., *The Book of Concord* (Philadelphia: Fortress, 1959), 19.
13. Paul Jersild, *Invitation to Faith* (Minneapolis: Augsburg, 1978), 130.
14. Joanne Marxhausen, *3 in 1* (St. Louis: Concordia, 1973).
15. Lewis, *Mere Christianity*, 141–42.
16. Harry Emerson Fosdick, "How Do You Picture God?" *Light for the Road*, eds. Samuel and Kathryn Rapport (New York: Harper & Row, 1961), 319.

Chapter 2

1. James Weldon Johnson, "The Creation," *Mindscapes: Poems for the Real World*, ed. Richard Pick (New York: Delacorte, 1971), 76.
2. C. S. Lewis, *Mere Christianity* (New York: Macmillan, 1943), 49–50.
3. John Vannorsdall, *Word and Doctrine* (Philadelphia: Lutheran Church Press, 1965), 10.
4. Jaroslav Pelikan, notes from "History of Doctrine" class at Yale Divinity School, 1966–67.
5. Tappert, *The Book of Concord*, 29.
6. Martin J. Heinecken, *We Believe and Teach* (Philadelphia: Fortress, 1980), 38–39.
7. Lesslie Newbigin, *Sin and Salvation* (Naperville, Ill.: SCM Book Club, 1956), 16–17.
8. Emil Brunner, *Our Faith* (London: SCM Press, 1949), 42.
9. Lewis, *Mere Christianity*, 70–71.
10. Jaroslav Pelikan, *Fools for Christ* (Philadelphia: Muhlenberg, 1955), 74.
11. Ron Sider, "Sin in the System," *Eerdmans' Handbook to Christian Belief*, ed. Robin Keeley (Grand Rapids: Eerdmans, 1982), 261.
12. *Lutheran Book of Worship* (Minneapolis: Augsburg, 1978), 56.
13. Paul Tillich, *The Shaking of the Foundations* (New York: Scribner's, 1948), 19.
14. Ruth Etchalls, "The Human Dilemma in Modern Literature," as quoted in Eerdman's *Handbook to Christian Belief*, ed. Robin Keeley (Grand Rapids: Eerdmans, 1982), 25.
15. Herbert Mowrer, *The Crisis in Psychiatry and Religion* (Princeton, N.J.: Van Nostrand, 1961), 54–55.
16. Arthur Miller, *After the Fall* (New York: Viking, 1964), 3–4.

17. Aleksandr I. Solzhenitsyn, *The Gulag Archipelago* (New York: Harper & Row, 1973), 168.

Chapter 3

1. William Barclay, *A New Testament Word Book* (New York: Harper, 1961), 111.
2. Tertullian, *Apologeticus* (Cambridge: n.p., 1917), 145.
3. George Forell, *The Protestant Faith* (Philadelphia: Fortress, 1960), 178–179.
4. Gabriel Fackre, *The Christian Story* (Grand Rapids: Eerdmans, 1978), 118.
5. Martin J. Heinecken, *We Believe and Teach* (Philadelphia: Fortress, 1980), 76–77.
6. "Table Talk," as quoted by Hugh T. Ken, Jr., ed., *The Compend of Luther's Theology* (Philadelphia: DeAmnster, 1943), 53.
7. *Lutheran Book of Worship* (Minneapolis: Augsburg, 1978), 123.
8. C. S. Lewis, *The Screwtape Letters* (New York: Macmillan, 1961), vii.
9. *Lutheran Book of Worship*, 229.
10. Reinhold Seeberg, *Textbook of the History of Doctrines*, trans. Charles Hay, vol. 1 (Philadelphia: Lutheran Publication Society, 1905), 71.
11. *Lutheran Book of Worship*, 482.
12. Daniel Erlander, *Baptized We Live* (Albuquerque: Hosanna, 1981), 4–5.
13. Harvey Cox, *The Secular City* (New York: Macmillan, 1965), 57.
14. Karl Barth, *Church Dogmatics*, vol. IV-2 (Edinburgh: T. & T. Clark, 1958), 20–153.
15. Gilbert E. Doan, Jr., "A Perspective on the Ascension," *Renewal in the Pulpit* (Philadelphia: Fortress, 1966), 138.

Chapter 4

1. Paul Tournier, *The Meaning of Gifts* (Atlanta: John Knox, 1966), 53.
2. Rolf Aaseng, *Basic Christian Teachings* (Minneapolis: Augsburg, 1982), 34.
3. William Streng, *Faith for Today* (Minneapolis: Augsburg, 1975), 51–52.
4. Søren Kierkegaard, *Philosophical Fragments* (Princeton, N.J.: Princeton University Press, 1962), 61–66.
5. David H. Read, *The Christian Faith* (New York: Scribner, 1956), 13.

6. Charles Anderson, *Faith and Freedom* (Minneapolis: Augsburg, 1977), 50.

7. Martin Luther, *The Small Catechism* (Minneapolis: Augsburg, 1968), 13.

8. Gabriel Fackre, *The Christian Story* (Grand Rapids: Eerdmans, 1978), 186.

9. Carl Krieg, *What to Believe: The Questions of Christian Faith* (Philadelphia: Fortress, 1974), 78.

10. Hugh T. Ken, Jr., ed., *The Compend of Luther's Theology* (Philadelphia: DeAmnster, 1943), 104.

11. Theodore Tappert, ed. and trans., *The Book of Concord* (Philadelphia: Fortress, 1959), 31–32.

12. George Forell, *The Augsburg Confession: A Contemporary Commentary* (Minneapolis: Augsburg, 1968), 32–33.

13. Tappert, ed., *The Book of Concord*, 345.

14. Robert Herhold, *Moments of Grace* (Philadelphia: Fortress, 1981), 10–11.

15. Frederick Buechner, as quoted in *Why Not?* (St. Louis: United Ministry in Higher Education Publications, 1968), 12.

16. John Vannorsdall, *Freedom* (Rock Island, Ill.: Board of Publication, Lutheran Church in America, n.d.).

17. Michel Quoist, *Prayers* (New York: Sheed and Ward, 1963), 11.

18. Thomas Woodward, *Turning Things Upside Down* (New York: Seabury, 1975), 49–50.

19. Martin Luther, *Luther's Works*, vol. 51 (Philadelphia: Muhlenberg, 1959), 51.

20. Luther, *The Small Catechism*, 5.

21. Luther, *Luther's Works*, vol. 31, 344.

22. Ibid.

23. Robert Jenson, *Story and Promise* (Philadelphia: Fortress, 1973), 98.

24. The Word, for Luther, was first Jesus, and second, the Bible.

25. As quoted in Robert Raines, *Creative Brooding* (New York: Macmillan, 1966), 102–3.

Chapter 5

1. Dietrich Bonhoeffer, *Life Together* (New York: Harper, 1954), 39. (See all of chapter 1.)

2. Theodore Tappert, ed. and trans., *The Book of Concord* (Philadelphia: Fortress, 1959), 32.
3. Robert Jenson, *Story and Promise* (Philadelphia: Fortress, 1973), 194.
4. Ibid., 7.
5. Elton Trueblood, *Company of the Committed* (New York: Harper & Row, 1961), 64.
6. Ibid., 45.
7. George Macleod, *Only One Way Left* (Glasglow, Scotland: The Iona Community, n.d.), 38.
8. *Lutheran Book of Worship* (Minneapolis: Augsburg, 1978), 122.
9. Martin Luther, *The Small Catechism* (Minneapolis: Augsburg, 1968), 25.
10. Tappert, *The Book of Concord*, 442–43.
11. A conflation of the texts from 1 Corinthians 11:23–25, Matthew 26:26–28, Mark 14:22–24, and Luke 22:19–20. From Tappert, *The Book of Concord*, 351.
12. American Lutheran Church–Lutheran Church in America, *A Statement on Communion Practices* (Minneapolis: Augsburg, 1978), 4.
13. Gregory Dix, *The Shape of the Liturgy* (London: Dacre, 1945), 744.
14. Thomas Woodward, *Turning Things Upside Down* (New York: Seabury, 1975), 66.
15. Frederick Denison Maurice, as quoted in Samuel M. Shoemaker, *With the Holy Spirit and With Fire* (New York: Harper & Row, 1960), 8.
16. Luther, *The Small Catechism*, 19.
17. Ronald Sider, *Rich Christians in an Age of Hunger* (Downers Grove, Ill.: InterVarsity Press, 1977), 33.
18. John and Mary Schramm, *Things That Make for Peace* (Minneapolis: Augsburg, 1976), 99.

Chapter 6

1. Henri Nouwen, "A Spirituality of Waiting," *The Weavings Reader: Living with God in the World* (Nashville: The Upper Room, 1993), 67.
2. Henri Nouwen, *Making All Things New* (San Francisco: Harper & Row, 1981), 72–73.
3. Told by Strother A. Campell, *Grit to Grapple with Life* (Nashville: The Broadman Press, 1942), 35.

4. Daniel Erlander, *Baptized We Live* (Albuquerque: Hosanna, 1981), 11–12.
5. Dietrich Bonhoeffer, *Life Together* (New York: Harper, 1954), 82.
6. Martin Luther, *Luther's Works*, American Edition, vol. 21 (St. Louis: Concordia, 1956), 140.
7. Other psalms pray for things for which we find it difficult to pray. Their lessons are for another time.

Chapter 7

1. Viktor E. Frankl, *Man's Search for Meaning* (New York: Pocket Books, 1959), 117–118.
2. Hans Schwartz, *On the Way to the Future* (Minneapolis: Augsburg, 1979), 162.
3. Robin Keeley, ed., *Eerdmans' Handbook to Christian Belief* (Grand Rapids: Eerdmans, 1982), 417.
4. Ibid., 412.
5. David Redding, *The Faith of Our Fathers* (Grand Rapids: Eerdmans, 1971), 92–93.
6. G. K. Chesterton, *Orthodoxy* (London: Fontana, 1908), 134–35.
7. Helmut Thielicke, *I Believe: The Christians' Creed* (Philadelphia: Fortress, 1968), 127.
8. Ibid., 124.

Chapter 8

1. Theodore Tappert, ed. and trans., *The Book of Concord* (Philadelphia: Fortress, 1959), 464.
2. Alan Richardson, "Authority of Scripture," *Interpreter's Dictionary of the Bible*, vol. 4 (Nashville: Abingdon, 1962), 250–251.
3. As quoted in Paul Little, *Know Why You Believe* (Wheaton, Ill.: Victor, 1977), 77.
4. Charles Anderson, *Faith and Freedom* (Minneapolis: Augsburg, 1977), 31.
5. Paul Tournier, *The Meaning of Gifts* (Atlanta: John Knox, 1966), 57.